UNDER THE RAINBOW

Published by WordCrafts Press
Cody, Wyoming 82414
www.wordcrafts.net

UNDER

THE

RAINBOW

The Exclusive True Story Behind The Stolen Ruby Slippers,
The Most Expensive Prop In Hollywood History,
And Who To Thank For Their Recovery

JEFF KEENE II

WordCrafts

To the Insabella Family,
who always remember,
blood is thicker than water.

To the pursuit of veracity.

"The truth is great and will prevail if left to herself."
~Thomas Jefferson

CONTENTS

DISCLAIMER

This book is not an attempt to replicate the fine research done and literature created by those who came before me regarding the renowned ruby slippers. My goal is not to provide the particulars a fan would love about *The Wizard of Oz* movie-making lore, nor to delve into the fine details of those persons involved with the ruby slippers before the 21st Century. Nor will I endeavor to deliver a biography of Judy Garland, all of which has been exhaustingly covered by previous authors and investigative reporters with exemplary credentials in their fields. Well done.

The purpose of this volume is to introduce the reader to the true story of one particular pair of shoes—the "traveling pair." Yes, there were five pairs, but this narrative focuses on the most infamous. How, and by whom, did these shoes move through the past century? And what mischievous havoc have these ruby slippers wrought upon those who coveted them as a possession or simply focused their thoughts upon their sequined brilliance, for good or for bad.

Reader beware.
Many believe this pair of slippers is cursed.

FOREWORD

U*nder the Rainbow* is an intriguing book about one pair of iconic ruby slippers worn by Judy Garland (Dorothy) in the classical 1939 film, *The Wizard of Oz.* But why would a book about that specific pair of shoes that Dorothy wore when she clicked her heels together three times be of enough interest to warrant reading this story? Because, in some respects, this book isn't really about the ruby shoes at all. It's about human behavior. How could a pair of tiny red slippers, that could not have cost more than a few dollars to make, now be worth several million? And what was the underworld, the dark side of human nature, willing to do to gain possession of those ruby slippers?

The book's author, who I personally know, spent countless hours doing research about the *path* of the ruby slippers over the last 83 years, and I believe you will find the story to be a fascinating one. One particularly interesting aspect the author's research has discovered is the personal tragedies that happened to all the people attempting to gain fame or fortune by acquiring or using Dorothy's fabled magical shoes.

But in the end, this book is about the motive, character, and integrity of a former United States Secret Service agent, Michael Insabella, who served on the White House security detail protecting three of our nation's Presidents: Ford, Carter, and Reagan.

ix

Through his close friendship with a famed criminal defense attorney, Insabella was asked to use his investigative skills and experience to assist in locating the ruby slippers stolen from a museum in Grand Rapids, Minnesota, in an unsolved burglary in 2005.

As a former Chairman and CEO of Office Depot, and now a minister, I had the privilege of getting to know Mike, both personally and professionally for more than three years when he was the Director of Executive Protection at Office Depot. During that time, his primary assignment was to plan and carry out security protection for me when traveling to high profile corporate meetings and events throughout the US, Europe, the UK, and Japan. During those three years we spent hundreds of hours together traveling. It was during that time that Mike gained my unwavering trust and confidence in his professionalism and competence. I have never known anyone in my life with more integrity, character, and honesty than Michael Insabella. Period.

The stolen pair of the ruby slippers were recovered several years ago due in no small part to the efforts and investigative work of Mike. Yet to this day, the FBI has slandered his name by insinuating he tried to extort money from an insurance company and by maintaining their perception and assumption that he was involved in a criminal act.

Nothing, could be further from the truth. As I previously stated, I know Mike very, very well. We now have a close personal relationship that has spanned more than twenty years since I left Office Depot. I know his entire family, his values, and of his belief and faith in God. I have never met anyone who keeps more precise and meticulous written records of important details, conversations, and emails.

I have been aware, for a long time, of the motive behind his desire to get the ruby slippers returned to the public view and not to some incredibly wealthy collector. He wanted the many followers of the classic and beloved film to be able to view the shoes and enjoy their long and storied history. All his intentions were honorable. His integrity is simply impeccable. To imply otherwise is a lie. The truth is in the pages of this book.

~Bruce Nelson
former Chairman and CEO of Office Depot

Mama Needs a New Pair of Shoes

No one really knows the full story of how the iconic ruby slippers were stolen on that fateful night of August 28, 2005. The perpetrators went unidentified for many years leaving the mystery unsolved for almost two decades.

Then the shoes were recovered in 2018.

This writer exposes what happened in the 13 years between the theft and their recovery by linking factual evidence, an exclusive interview, and a myriad of news reports all to be revealed in the succeeding chapters of this book.

But for now, as for the theft itself, it may have gone down something like this . . .

"This should be an easy job, in and out. Drive for three hours, grab the slippers, and drive back to Ham Lake in time for breakfast."

Kent Anderson chuckled as he popped a pistachio nut into his mouth. "Punching the lock to that gallery was a lot easier than crackin' any safe. Not supposed to be any safes tonight." He snorted as he crunched the nut's shell between his teeth. And he wouldn't shut up about his previous nefarious escapades. "We sure made a mess of those people's lives back in Edina. Nobody should miss these ruby slippers like that artwork. Can you believe they found those stupid paintings down in South America just a few years ago? The money we made on that heist is long gone."

He elbowed Carl. The two men spent the nearly three-hour drive from Ham Lake, Minnesota, to Grand Rapids, Minnesota, in a constant one-way conversation. And Kent was the one who couldn't keep his mouth shut. The idiot talked for the entire trip. He didn't even stop for a breath. On and on, story after story, each one more stupid than the previous. Carl bided his time as he drove. He looked at the radio's clock and sighed. The green LED lights shone back at him. Fifteen minutes past midnight. *Nearly an hour left of this guy.* He sighed. *Ugh, then the trip back.*

Carl forced a dry laugh in response to a quip Kent just said. "Yeah, you're real funny."

"If you think I'm funny, you should hear my brother, Louie. He's the comedian in the family." Kent chuckled then whispered mockingly to Carl. "But everyone says I'm funnier." He rolled the window partially down and spit a pistachio shell from his scruffy face.

How can I get this guy to shut up? "You know, we'll be at the place in 'bout an hour. Why not get some shuteye?"

Kent ignored the suggestion. "My brother . . ." He shook his head. "I'm trying to imagine what he'd think if he knew what we were about to do."

"Oh, yeah? You're not thinking of telling him, are you?"

"Are you nuts? That fat jerk would probably want them for himself!"

Carl looked askance at Kent. "He'd want a pair of ladies shoes for himself?"

"Let's just say," he spit another shell then rolled up the window, "he's a supporter of their cause."

"Whose cause?"

"The shoes were Judy Garland's. The gays? They loved her."

"You sayin' your brother's queer?"

"He's a professional comedian. It doesn't matter what he is, as long as he keeps sending me checks!" He laughed loudly. "Say, I'm

2

gonna take you up on that shuteye." Kent rolled to the right and rested his head on the window. "Wake me when we roll into town."

Carl grunted in agreement.

Kent shifted in his seat. "Oh, and it's the Grand Rapids in *this* state. I don't wanna wake up in no Michigan."

Forty-five minutes later, the men entered Judy Garland's hometown. Carl cut the engine of the aging, white Chevy Lumina, turned off the headlights, and rolled into the parking lot of the museum. Other than the colorful signs, muted by late night shadows, it looked as if they'd pulled up to someone's house.

Garland's old childhood home stood in front of the men through the car's windshield. The main museum building lay to the right. Their target entryway stood on the south side facing the historic home.

Just as we were told.

With baseball bats in hand, the men exited into the dark property and slithered along the wall under the cover of a row of short evergreen trees.

Kent eyed the window, scanned their surroundings, and drew his arm back.

"Wait." Carl's coarse whisper echoed off Garland's home. "The alarm."

"*Pfft.* What alarm?"

Crash!

Glass spilled from the door's broken window in tiny pieces that reflected the red light from the interior exit sign as they bounced onto the floor of the hallway.

Kent reached in and pushed the bar releasing the latch.

Three seconds later, Carl stood in the building alone. He turned to Kent. "A quick right turn, isn't that what he said?"

Kent nodded once then turned to scan the parking lot again.

Carl turned the knob and the door to the darkened gallery creaked open.

Unlocked? No guard?

The pedestal holding their prize stood on the floor in front of him while the other displays and Hollywood artifacts in his periphery went black. His focus was singular.

My turn.

Carl strode forward making a beeline for the ruby slippers. He raised his bat and let if fall onto the plexiglass case without hesitation. Shards of the clear material fell about his feet onto the linoleum tiled floor.

He grabbed the shoes with gloved hands and thrust them into a small canvas duffle bag. One shoe rubbed on the zipper sloughing off a single ruby-colored sequin.

As the dark red disk, the width of a pencil's eraser, tumbled through the air, Carl made his way out of the museum. The entire caper took a mere 45 seconds to carry out.

Kent spoke first once they were back in the car and on the road headed south. "Well, that was the easiest job I've ever pulled off."

"Yea, for *you*. You were the lookout." Carl looked into the rearview mirror to scan the road behind them for flashing lights. He shifted in his seat. "They can't be worth that much with no alarm. That was too easy."

Kent leaned back and relaxed after placing the duffel bag on the back seat. "Yea, I've seen better security when they knew my brother was going to the buffet line."

Carl snorted. "Now *that* was funny."

Perhaps that's how it happened. We may never know. Read on and determine for yourself.

PART 1

CHAPTER 1

THE SHOES COME TO LIFE

Consider the classic and beloved family film, *The Wizard of Oz*. Few Hollywood creations, particularly of that era, conjure such fervent memories in children of all ages and from all over the world. The visions linger long into adulthood.

Who, from almost any walk of life, can't recall the scenes that stand out to them most? From the terrifying twister and flying monkeys to the Munchkins and magical ruby slippers, the spectacle of magnificent cinematic events and props seemed unending. Quotes from the film are infused into the fabric of society. From, "We're not in Kansas anymore," to "Lions and tigers and bears. Oh, my," these references resurface time and again in movies, television shows, books, and print media. Hardly a week goes by without seeing an allusion to "There's no place like home" or some other Oz-esque paraphrase.

But it's this last incantation that brought those ruby slippers to life—when Dorothy clicked her heels together three times—showing everyone their true power. The shoes, out of all the items in the movie, were what everyone had their eyes on. Their mysterious nature and brilliant sparkle drew audience members into the screen and transported them into the Land of Oz. Unknown to many of these movie fans, that fictional magical quality crossed over into reality, and with a sinfulness that would put a smile on the face of the Wicked Witch of the West herself.

The ruby slippers were fought over by the main characters so much that the concepts of theft, kidnapping, and even threats of murder have been intertwined into their story. Those concepts lived on for nearly 85 years weaving a conspiracy so convoluted that a new blockbuster movie or hit television series could readily be created. But what vexations would plague the players in this new production? What novel trials would the actors, directors, and crew endure for daring to play a part in the story of the mystery behind the infamous ruby slippers?

In the spring of 1900, a children's story written by L. Frank Baum was published titled, *The Wonderful Wizard of Oz*. It introduced the world to many unheard of enchantments. Baum stated in an introductory passage to his book, "It aspires to being a modernized fairy tale, in which the wonderment and joy are retained and the heart-aches and nightmares are left out." But there are many today who could recount tales of their nocturnal dreamscapes being fueled by a cackling witch and a grove of groping apple trees. And there are many others who, in the following pages, will be revealed as having undergone those nightmares in their waking hours. And all driven by the lure of the ruby slippers. To find and to hide, to possess and to sell, to bring joy to others and to bring justice for all.

Original cover of L. Frank Baum's
The Wonderful Wizard of Oz

In Baum's book, the ruby slippers weren't slippers at all and they were most certainly not studded with sparkling precious stones. They were portrayed as pointed shoes of silver. And Dorothy E. Gale placed them on her feet all by herself, with their magic only hinted to before striking off on her yellow-brick-road adventure with the cowardly lion, tin man, and scarecrow.

Thirty-nine years later, Hollywood changed all that in the movie version with a curtailed title, *The Wizard of Oz*. On page 26 of the script, scene #113, in line 109A, the word "*silver*" was scratched out. A screenwriter had written "*ruby*" above it. This was done to avoid the shoes being washed out on the big screen by the new Technicolor lighting. As a matter of fact, all the colors on set were much darker in reality, from Dorothy's dress to the Munchkin uniforms. So, they cast the slippers as jeweled pumps covered with red fabric, painted red soles, dark red sequins, and bows of stiff cotton. Glass beads and rhinestones created the shimmering on-screen effect which made audiences gasp as the shoes wondrously teleported from the deceased Wicked Witch of the East's curled toes onto Dorothy's size five-and-a-half feet.

The slippers didn't start off as the ones seen on screen, however. Rarely in Hollywood productions do props and costumes go from page to stage without alterations. Take Darth Vader's helmet. After the initial plan made of sculpted clay was fashioned to look like a futuristic Nazi helmet, many designs came forth on paper until the 1977 *Star Wars: A New Hope* version appeared on the big screen. And in every movie and television series since, that costume can still be seen evolving.

The Arabian test pair at auction in 2011

These slippers proved no different. Gilbert Adrian, commonly known simply as "Adrian" at the time, was a costumer working on the movie for Metro-Goldwyn-Mayer Studios. He had been charged with determining the style of ruby slippers Judy Garland would wear when filming. The original pair of shoes looked more like something a Christmas elf would don when building toys in Santa's workshop. This experimental pair, better known as the "Arabian test pair," evolved under Adrian's watchful care from that elfish style to simple pumps without bows to what we know and love in the movie.

And it was these final creations, of which several pairs were worn by Garland, that carried the actress across the soundstage and into cinematic history. Because of their pivotal meaning in the story and gripping allure to fans, they are widely considered to be one of the most recognizable pieces of memorabilia in American film history and estimated today to be worth several million dollars.

Which makes it even more interesting to discover that on August 28, 2005, 73 years and three days after the movie debuted, this "traveling pair" of ruby slippers disappeared.

And not for the first time.

One of the few pairs of ruby slippers from The Wizard of Oz.

CHAPTER 2

THE SHOES TAKE FLIGHT

Immediately after production of *The Wizard of Oz* and the release of the film in 1939, Metro-Goldwyn-Mayer Studios, Incorporated, placed everything, from the scarecrow costume and Winkie spears to Dorothy's blue and white, gingham pinafore dress and the—what are assumed to be—multiple pairs of ruby slippers into deep storage for 30 years.

Then, in 1970, the entire studio sold to a reclusive financier named Kerkor "Kirk" Kerkorian. He turned around and liquidated all the props and property to finance a Las Vegas casino, the MGM Grand. He sold the studio land and backlot props, and started to decimate MGM's closet full of antiques, artwork, machinery, and costumes.

Fortunately, he sold the bulk of the items to an auctioneer named David Weisz. The David Weisz Company bought all of MGM's costumes for something like a dollar apiece and had initially planned a bazaar sale direct to the public for prices just above that. Greater than 350,000 items were in that gigantic closet, and the auction was set to commence on May 1st and remain open for 17 days.

Among the multitude of items placed under the gavel were over 300,000 costumes, furniture and decorative-art related items, automobiles, busses, trains, tanks, boats, ships, airplanes, and space

MGM auction props, 1970

capsules that were previously incorporated into studio productions. Some of the highlights were the full-size sailing ship from *Mutiny on the Bounty* (1935), Elizabeth Taylor's wedding gown worn in *Father of the Bride* (1950), Clark Gable's trench coat from several films, a group of swimsuits worn by Esther Williams, and Johnny Weissmuller's loin cloth worn in 1940s Tarzan flicks. However, the most coveted pieces sold were from *The Wizard of Oz* production.

Each day, more than 6,000 people paid $100 dollars for admittance to this series of auctions that lasted over three weeks. The crowd included professional decorators, antiques dealers, amateur collectors seeking a modest possession with MGM status, and Hollywood people looking for mementos from MGM's more majestic days. Rock Hudson, Nanette Fabray, and Shirley Jones were among the celebrities present.

Weisz hired a Hollywood costumer by the name of Kent Warner. Kent came to be known as the "Robin Hood of Hollywood." From

12

1964 to 1972, Warner recognized the atrocities occurring throughout Hollywood's studios. Whole racks of costumes were just thrown away or burned in great dumpster bonfires. Out with the old was the studios' motto, but Warner saw things differently. He wanted to preserve items like the dresses from *Gone with the Wind* and John Wayne's boots. He recognized these important pieces and traveled from backlot to backlot gathering and saving what he could before it was too late. After all, everything was tagged and the pickings proved numerous.

Having been hired to help with the MGM auction, Warner decided to take costumes in lieu of payment. And he took that offer to the nth degree. He scoured the backlots and searched every closet, trailer, and shed. At one point, he found a decrepit barn in the back of a lot. After initially surveying all in his sight, he climbed into a loft labeled "3rd Floor – Ladies Character Wardrobe." He recalls it as being hot, smelly, and dark. "A ray of sunlight reflected off a sequin. I walked over. I didn't touch them. The red and the sequins appeared, and I knew they were the ruby slippers."

He found all the slippers, including the "Arabian test pair," and took them home to examine them. He wanted to determine which were used in the movie, in what scenes, and for what purpose. Of the pairs Warner confessed to finding, he kept the "witch's shoes" for his own personal collection. These were the close-up shoes, as they didn't have red felt on the bottom. The felt would have been used on pairs

MGM David Weisz Wardrobe catalog cover

13

Judy Garland wore to prevent loud clacking on the yellow-brick road, which was actually made of plywood on the movie set. In a later newspaper article, Kent Warner was quoted as saying, "I'm the only person in the world that knows the story of the ruby slippers ...I discovered the ruby slippers."

But let's take a step back. Whatever Warner found in the *Wizard of Oz* ruby slipper stash in that loft was at least for certain one pair short. One of the pairs made for the movie had been awarded to a Miss Roberta Bauman of Memphis, Tennessee, immediately after the movie's release 30 years before. At that time, she was a high school student who had written an essay in an effort to win an unknown prize from the studio. It turns out that prize was a genuine pair of Dorothy's ruby slippers! She held on to that pair, which have come to be known as "Dorothy's shoes," for nearly 50 years before parting with them.

So, what did Kent Warner do with the other pairs of shoes he found in that dark and dingy loft?

MGM ladies' wardrobe in the 1930s

14

Actress Debbie Reynolds

Only one pair was delivered to the MGM liquidators. He had let the auctioneer assume they were the only ones in existence. As far anyone knew, they were. Before the auction, Weisz purportedly ordered Warner to "destroy the other pairs or make them disappear" so as to increase their rarity and inflate the bidding. Warner was then tasked with parading the remaining pair up and down the platform as the auctioneer called off dollar amounts. He had perched them on a satin pillow for dramatic effect. In the end, they sold for $15,000. These shoes came to be known as the "dancing pair" or "people's shoes" and were eventually donated in 1979 to the Smithsonian National Museum of American History in Washington, D.C. to be put on perpetual display.

Perhaps you've been privileged enough to have seen them. Extensive scientific analysis of these shoes has taken place, down to the molecular structure of the sequins and red paint.[1]

The Arabian pair, never put up for auction, was sold privately by Warner to actress Debbie Reynolds for a purported diminutive sum of $300. She spent a fortune at that MGM auction in a valiant attempt at saving Hollywood artifacts from destruction and loss. She had planned to open a museum with all she purchased. It never came to be.

A fourth pair was sent by Warner to Michael Shaw, a collector of Silver Screen mementos, who paid $2,500 for them in 1970. At the time, these were the only pair known to have Judy Garland's name written inside. Shaw held on to this pair as part of a unique collection of memorabilia kept in his home. Eventually, he took much of it, including such items as the tablets and golden calf from Cecil B. DeMille's 1956 epic, *The Ten Commandments*, on tour around the country to places like shopping malls as part of a touring museum of Hollywood relics. After some years, he reduced his show to include only the *Wizard of Oz* items, one of which was his popular pair of ruby slippers, now known as the "traveling pair."

In 1980, Kent Warner had learned the one remaining pair of shoes in his possession had become more than he initially bargained for. Visitors were drawn to his home to see the shoes rather than to visit Warner. Their very presence made him uneasy, and they eventually lost their meaning. For him, the treasure's weight was more than he could bear. He listed his prized possession at a memorabilia auction in Los Angeles for $20,000. They did not sell. A year later, Warner let Christies Auction House in New York sell them. They went for a mere $12,600 to a mysterious bidder.

Tragically, Kent Warner passed away three years later of complications from AIDS. He was 41 years old.

At this point in our story, all five pairs of identified shoes had known whereabouts. The "witch's shoes" were sold at auction to an anonymous buyer, the "dancing pair" were safely ensconced in Washington, D.C., "Dorothy's shoes" sat in the care of an aging Roberta Bauman in Tennessee, the "traveling pair" were well-guarded by collector Michael Shaw, and the "Arabian pair" were equally well-protected in Debbie Reynolds' estate.

Perhaps the shoes should have been thrown into the trash or burned with the other movie treasures. Or were they cleverly created with malice to impact the lives of so many who came into contact with them? After all, orchestrations for the film and production files were dumped into a landfill and had a freeway built over them. The surviving outtakes, the screen tests, and all the original nitrate film were put on a barge and dumped in the Pacific Ocean.

Why had the shoes survived?

What happens to them all over the next 35e years has frustrated many souls. Investigative reporters, curators, auctioneers, and law enforcement officers have all been affected. In the end, maybe even this author will feel the force these magical shoes generate. Before it can be known, we must first look at some of that magic. Judge for yourself if it's the light or dark kind.

Publicity photo *The Wizard of Oz*

CHAPTER 3

THE SHOES CHOOSE THEIR OWN PATH

Can you imagine Roberta Bauman's surprise when she heard that she didn't own the only pair of ruby slippers from *The Wizard of Oz?* It's like spending your life savings on Tom Brady's last thrown football before he retired to only find out he un-retired and your football is now worth the price of a taco platter. That was probably her perception. But that was not Bauman's reality.

In 1988, Roberta Bauman did some research, and it paid off. She was, indeed, the holder of an official pair of ruby slippers used in the movie. And although she used them to bring joy to countless children and fans over their years in her possession, she felt it was time for them to depart. Perhaps they'd provide enough money for her to live well enough in her retirement. She contacted Julie Collier of Christies and put them up for auction. Lot #125. Listed as "Dorothy's shoes," the bidding started around the amount that Kent Warner's sold for seven years earlier, $12,000.

It did not take long for the bids to rise well above that number. Later, in a phone call from Collier to Bauman, Collier said, "It was the most exciting auction they ever held." According to Bauman, in reference to that phone call, Collier had gotten word that at one point even Ted Turner had bid on them. In the end, "Dorothy's shoes" ended up selling for $150,000. The shoes had found a new home with an elated collector by the name of Anthony Landini.

Later that same year, the "witch's shoes," Kent Warner's pair which sold at auction for a measly $12,500 in 1981, resurfaced. Perhaps the anonymous owners had gotten wind of the incredible sale price of Bauman's shoes, and it pressured them to sell while the selling was good. Julie Collier once again took charge of the sale, but this time there was no public auction. She found a collector in St. Louis, Missouri, by the name of Phillip Samuels. He paid $165,000 for Kent Warner's pair.

A year later, while riding her bicycle on the streets of Manhattan, Julie Collier was struck by a truck and tragically killed.

Over the years, Samuels loaned out the "witch's pair" to the Smithsonian when their pair needed to be removed from the display for maintenance. Over time, Phillip Samuels' son Albert Samuels took over ownership of this pair and eventually put them up for auction yet again in 2011. They expected the shoes to sell for between two and three million dollars. But they did not sell at auction. Instead, a private sale was again sought. It is rumored that big Hollywood players, so-called "angel donors," such as Leonardo DiCaprio, Stephen Spielberg, former Warner Brothers chairman Terry Semel, and others chipped in to purchase the "witch's pair" which were then donated to the Academy of Motion Picture Arts and Sciences in Los Angeles.

When received, Bob Iger, president and CEO of the Walt Disney Company and chair of the fundraising campaign for the Academy Museum of Motion Pictures, said in a statement, "The ruby slippers occupy an extraordinary place in the hearts of movie audiences the world over. This is a transformative acquisition for our collection."

A better place cannot be imagined in which to enshrine them.

Getting back to Anthony Landini's "Dorothy's pair"—he worked with Disney World's MGM Studios in Florida and made a deal to display the shoes at the Chinese Theatre reproduction's "Great Movie Ride." Here, they sat on a glass-enclosed pedestal surrounded by a velvet cord so millions of visitors could marvel at their mystery and uniqueness for years.

But, like the "one ring to rule them all" of *The Lord of the Rings* saga, the ruby slippers needed to move on and find a new owner. Landini eventually auctioned the "witch's pair" to a collector for $666,000. The collector was David Elkouby and his partners who own a series of memorabilia shops in Hollywood, California. Elkouby was heard saying, ". . .bring them back to Hollywood. We are working on a Hollywood museum." But since 2016, they have supposedly been locked in a bank vault, and no one has been given permission to view them. For all anyone knows, they were sold again to a private collector and now festoon an ornate shelf in a crystal glass case in the privacy of an opulent living room.

As for Debbie Reynolds' "Arabian pair," they spent some time on display in a museum in Las Vegas only to be ultimately sold by her, along with many pieces from her enormous collection, through auction in an effort to pay debts. In 2011, these shoes sold for $510,000, but that new owner remains a mystery to the public.

What did the ownership of these treasured footwear ever bring to anyone? It can be said that the only time the ruby slippers did anything positive was when they were used for the enjoyment of everyone. There are no reports about the people involved in museum curation, such as those at the Smithsonian, ever having untimely deaths. And Roberta Bauman, after enchanting children for 40 years by freely sharing the magic of her pair of slippers with them, was blessed with a long life and earlier than expected retirement. But whenever a pair were used for personal gain or coveted as a possession, the people involved usually suffered.

Perhaps a curse *was* placed upon them at their inception.

With all the historical drama on the set of *The Wizard of Oz*, one would doubt if someone hadn't jinxed them. Or maybe the spirit of the wicked sisters who squabbled over them on-screen had something to do with their vexation. And maybe that's where everything went wrong for Michael Shaw and his "traveling pair," the last and most intriguing ruby slipper story so far.

CHAPTER 4

THE SHOES' REBELLIOUS EXIT

The Judy Garland Museum in Grand Rapids, Minnesota, was founded in 1975 by artist Jacquilyn "Jackie" L. Dingmann. The simple reason being that Garland was born there in 1922. Updated in 2003, the museum houses the largest collection of Judy Garland memorabilia in the world. Part of the assemblage includes Garland's childhood historic home and the carriage, once belonging to President Abraham Lincoln, that was pulled by the polychromatic horse in *The Wizard of Oz*. In 2005, the museum was the temporary home of Michael Shaw's "traveling pair" of ruby slippers, as well.

Until they disappeared.

In a previous chapter, we learned that Shaw had spent years showing his pair of shoes across America for a fee and eventually they became the star attraction. Like Kent Warner, it's possible

The parking lot of the Judy Garland Museum in Grand Rapids, Minnesota

Shaw felt as if his ruby slippers had taken more of the spotlight than himself.

The shoes pulled at their owner's subconscious. They wanted change.

In 1989, and on subsequent occasions, Shaw lent the shoes to the Judy Garland Museum. When he first arrived with them, the media spectacle drew thousands of diehard fans from across the nation and even from other countries. During the extravaganza, Shaw's misguided attachment to his prized possession was made obvious during one heartbreaking encounter. A young girl with an undisclosed ailment resulting in blindness had traveled with her mother for many miles to touch the shoes. After witnessing the movie magic in the film, she believed they had actual healing powers and would make her see again. Fearing her touch would damage the already worn memorabilia and drive others to want to touch them too, Shaw flatly refused the little girl's dire request.

Eventually, in 2005, the museum paid Shaw about $5,500 to display the shoes for two months. They even flew him in to deliver them in person.

Before arriving, Shaw went to Minneapolis with the shoes to attend a library event and undergo an interview. This had the effect of letting everyone know exactly where and when the shoes would be exhibited. While there, the museum in Grand Rapids attempted to prepare for the treasure's arrival by ordering a vault from a local bank. Shaw refused their offer for the same reason he had forbidden the little girl. He didn't want people touching them. In a later interview, Shaw stated another rationalization for his rejection of a safe. He was under the impression the museum had security cameras and motion sensor alarms. He also believed the local police would make regular visits and check on the facility after hours.

The shoes went on display.

Placed on a wooden pedestal and covered by a plexiglass case, nothing more than a simple velvet-rope barrier guarded them.

On the contrary, when Roberta Bauman's pair went on exhibition at Disney's MGM Studio theme park in Bay Lake, Florida, in 1989, they received security guards and cameras. In Washington, D.C., the Smithsonian's ruby slippers sit among a guarded collection, in a gallery with manned video monitors and within an alarmed encasement. Shaw's shoes, after arriving in a small venue in Grand Rapids, Minnesota, had no such security. A responsible party had dropped the ball making simple work for an opportunistic villain.

The "Traveling Pair" of slippers at the Judy Garland Museum in Grand Rapids, Minnesota, before their theft in 2005.

But who was accountable? And who were the perpetrators? For when the shoes were stolen in the middle of the night on August 28, 2005, it appeared as if both could be one in the same.

"They had none of it. I never would have left the shoes if I knew there was such a lack of security." Shaw's statement is one made by many who plan insurance fraud. But there was no proof that he partook in such a scheme. Maybe it was the museum curator or an employee. After all, the alarm had been manually turned off, the cameras were only for monitoring and had never been set to record, and the door to the room where the shoes were displayed had been conveniently left unlocked. Certainly, Shaw could not have orchestrated such a myriad of coincidences from his residence 2,000 miles away in North Hollywood, California. It must have been an inside job. Right?

David Letterman joked in a monologue that week that "a pair of ruby red slippers worn by Judy Garland in *The Wizard of Oz* have been stolen. The thief is described as being armed and fabulous."

Some found it funny, but not the locals. And not the admirers of Judy Garland. An economy had been threatened, and an icon had been yanked away from fans.

After the initial investigation, it was determined that every chink in the museum's armor could be logically explained away and none there were found at fault. The slippers had been insured for $1 million, and Shaw walked away with a settlement of $800,000 for his loss. All the museum received for their loss was the opportunity to sweep up broken glass from the back door. To this day, it still suffers losses to its volume of annual visitors because its prized treasure went missing 17 years ago.

But where did the "traveling pair" of ruby slippers go? Were there clues left behind for investigators to trail the culprits? And who were the perpetrators of this dastardly wrongdoing? Many investigators have endeavored to find out. And some dedicated untold periods of time to this task.

CHAPTER 5

THE GHOSTS OF SHOES PAST

Conflicting reports about the stolen ruby slippers spread like wildfire through the small town of Grand Rapids, Minnesota. Rumors of their destruction and possible location kept the local detectives busy.

Conflicting perceptions about how well the authorities handled the case were rampant. According to Detective Andy Morgan, "Countless hours had been dedicated to tracking down the slippers." But the museum curator saw things differently. He stated, "They never took complete fingerprints," and "We never heard from the police department" after their initial visit.

From a distance, when Shaw heard about the incident, he claimed he was sick for three days and unable to travel. But in the end, he accepted the insurance company, Essex's, $800,000 payout and offer that he would have first dibs in purchasing them back if ever found.

Years passed, and the case, never warm to begin with, had grown icy cold. Only one piece of evidence had been found at the museum that night: a single red sequin had fallen off one of the shoes. Originally collected and placed into evidence by Grand Rapids detectives, today it is not publicly known where that sequin is. It is presumed to be in the custody of the FBI.

On the ten year anniversary of the theft, the Judy Garland

Museum hired a private investigator to delve into the case. Rob Feeney identified himself as the "least qualified person for this" task but took on the case with gusto.

Feeney pleaded with the FBI to get them involved. But they confessed their disinterest due to the expired statute of limitations. There was no one to arrest, regardless of the evidence. Even though, according to Feeney, he had made progress over the first eight months he was on the case. The suspects have been narrowed down to two young men, Feeney said. "We believe the suspects are local," he added. What came of that lead has not been uncovered.

Tips trickled in about the shoes over the next decade. In 2015, Detective Brian Mattson, who had taken over the cold case from a previous investigator, received a report that the shoes were sealed in a paint can and thrown into a local mining pit, long abandoned and now filled with water hundreds of feet deep. This lead, along with many other similar ones over the years, were found to be false after divers were dispatched each time and came up empty handed.

Yet other reports of the theft involved wild stories varying from drug underworld goons to celebrity relatives gone bad. A community of master thieves in the Minneapolis underground sounds like something out of a bad novel. But, as with much about this story, the truth is stranger than fiction. And, with the inclusion of both these reports, the sordid plot thickened. To muddle through it all, we'll need to go back in time 26 years before the shoes were stolen.

In 1979, seven paintings of the American painter and illustrator Norman Rockwell and a forged Renoir were stolen from the Elayne Galleries in Edina, a suburb of Minneapolis. In a 2013 book about the theft by local journalist Bruce Rubenstein titled *The Rockwell Heist*, he declined to name three of the four robbers who were still living at the time. But actor Louie Anderson's brother Kent Anderson, who died in 2007, was named as one of them. It had been the biggest theft in Minnesota history, and no one was ever convicted of the crime.

When the ruby slipper case stalled, Detective Mattson called in a contact, Chris Dudley, from the Federal Bureau of Investigation to help. Since Rubinstein had named Kent Anderson as one of four in the Rockwell heist, the FBI wanted to talk to Rubinstein about the ruby slippers. After all, this theft now passed the Rockwell paintings in dollar amount by hundreds of thousands if not millions of dollars. Due to the high-profile artifacts and the proximity of the crimes to each other, Dudley thought there might be a connection between the two.

In the interview with Rubinstein, the journalist asked, "What's in it for me?" For whatever reason, Rubinstein did not want to help the FBI. The agents pressured Rubenstein during their interview with him. They wanted to know if he had any information worth knowing that could tie these two thefts together. Finally, he told them he thought the shoes and the Rockwell thefts may have been connected.

During Rubenstein's research, he asked a contact if there was anyone in the field crazy enough to want the slippers. The contact informed him that in Brentwood, California, there was a garage behind a home where one could see the slippers—for a price. Had the shoes found their way back to the West Coast? If Kent Anderson had been involved in the Rockwell heist, what would a gangster know about *Wizard of Oz* memorabilia? Perhaps, because his brother was a famous actor, he got wind of the opportunity and took action. But Kent was 70 years old in 2005. Did he turn to a local connection ("Carl" in the Prologue) in Grand Rapids to commit the

Actor/Comedian Louie Anderson,
brother of suspect Kent Anderson.

crime, as some people suggested? If so, it's possible the shoes traded hands several times through an underground market and ended up there in California. An investigation found the garage empty. And the existence of that pair was never confirmed. So, the FBI continued to push.

Rubenstein then mentioned the name of a defense lawyer, Joe Friedberg, "the patriarch of criminal defense of the Twin Cities" as an interesting party. He had been a source in Rubenstein's own investigation of the Rockwell heist, but only because Friedberg had refused to represent the thieves so long ago. Could Friedberg know anything about this theft? The tenuous ties holding this investigation together seemed to be fraying.

Even early on, Joe Friedberg seemed to know more than he was sharing. But did he have a choice? Lawyers are famous for referencing and putting to practice the attorney-client privilege. This refers to the legal entitlement that works to keep confidential communications between an attorney and their clients confidential. The privilege is asserted in the face of a legal petition for communications, such as a discovery request or a demand that the lawyer testify under oath.

Friedberg had close ties to leaders in the crime syndicate. After all, he was a high-profile defense attorney. This makes sense. But as with many people's line of work, it's not what you know but who you know. And Friedberg knew some low-life individuals. Some of the acquaintances of those individuals took it upon themselves to pay visits to Friedberg's office from time to time, as his reputation for being helpful preceded him. Friedberg didn't like it.

Robert Wittman, the FBI agent who started the art crimes unit in 2004, a year before the slippers were stolen, has been quoted as saying, "The real art in an art heist isn't the stealing, it's the selling," and most thieves are nabbed trying to resell the ill-gotten treasures. One method to avoid being caught is to wait until the statute of limitations has run out then attempt to extort the owners or the insurers for the safe return of the property using a middleman, sometimes a lawyer. As a top Minneapolis criminal-defense attorney, Friedberg told Rubenstein he was approached about just such a deal regarding the Rockwell paintings a few years after their theft. According to Rubenstein, a man asked Friedberg to help negotiate the paintings' return. That man wanted Friedberg to talk with the insurance company on his behalf for the reward money. Rubenstein wrote, "Friedberg asked the State Professional Responsibility Board if it was ethical to do what the caller proposed." Friedberg told the board that the art might be destroyed, which is a common threat made in art crime extortion. Friedberg was advised it could be considered a felony to aid in the return of the Rockwell paintings. He then told Rubenstein, "I passed."

Another incident involved a missing Fabergé egg. The Third Imperial Easter Egg, to be exact.

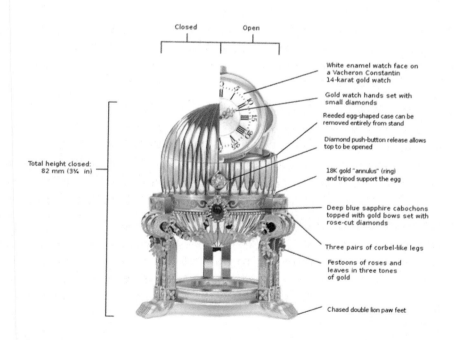

White enamel watch face on a Vacheron Constantin 14-karat gold watch

Gold watch hands set with small diamonds

Reeded egg-shaped case can be removed entirely from stand

Diamond push-button release allows top to be opened

18K gold "annulus" (ring) and tripod support the egg

Deep blue sapphire cabochons topped with gold bows set with rose-cut diamonds

Three pairs of corbel-like legs

Festoons of roses and leaves in three tones of gold

Chased double lion paw feet

Closed   Open

Total height closed: 82 mm (3¼ in)

The Third Imperial Easter Egg, dated 1887.

This piece of art is a jeweled and ridged yellow-gold egg sitting on a tripod pedestal. It stands on embossed lion paw feet and is encircled by colored gold garlands suspended from blue cabochon sapphires. It is topped with rose diamond-set bows. In the traditional Fabergé style, the egg contains a surprise—a lady's watch by Vacheron Constantin, with a white enamel dial and openwork diamond-set gold hands. The egg was first given by Russian Emperor Alexander III to Empress Marie Feodorovna for Easter in 1887. Estimated price? $33 million. The egg had been lost for decades and has not been publicly seen since 1903.

But how did this famous treasure end up in the hands of a Midwest American scrap metal dealer? And what does this have to do with Joe Friedberg and the ruby slippers?

According to Mark Westall, in a Fad Magazine article dated September 2021, the egg appeared at an auction in New York in 1964 but was unrecognized. It then disappeared until 2011, when it was bought for its gold weight value of $14,000 at a Midwest flea market.

Soon after, in that same year, this Midwestern man approached Kieran McCarthy of Wartski Jewelers in London with pictures of the Fabergé egg.

According to a 2014 Artnet article written by Daniella LaGaccia:

The man, who said the egg was resting on his kitchen counter, originally bought it from an antiques store in the Midwest; unaware of its value, he had planned to melt down the priceless antique for its gold and the diamonds and sapphires attached to its surface.

In 2012, after the object had been languishing on his counter for years, the man Google-searched the word "egg" and the name inscribed on the object, "Vacheron Constantin," and found a newspaper article referring to the lost jewel. The man said he immediately contacted Fabergé expert Kieran McCarthy of jeweler Wartski, who later confirmed its authenticity. Wartski bought the egg on behalf of a collector.

"The second I saw it, my spine was shivering," McCarthy told the Associated Press, before calling the piece the "Holy Grail" for collectors. McCarthy subsequently set up a buyer for the egg, and while he didn't disclose the sale price or the identity of the buyer, experts have noted that a non-imperial Fabergé egg sold at Christie's for $18.5 million in 2007.

In a June 2015 CNN article, Susannah Cullinane wrote:

McCarthy said he had no warning about the visit.

"A gentleman had walked in wearing jeans, a plaid shirt, and trainers. His mouth was just dry with fear," McCarthy said, to the extent that he could barely speak. "He handed me a portfolio of photographs, and there was the egg, the Holy Grail of art and antiques."

Though he had not handled the egg itself, McCarthy said, he was "buzzing from top to toe." He flew to the man's home to see the object in person and confirmed that it was indeed the Third Imperial Egg.

The finder "just can't believe his luck," McCarthy said. "It's almost an affirmation of his existence that this happened to him."

The finder was far removed from the art and antiques world and so had not recognized the object's true value.

"He didn't look upon it as a work of art at all. He saw that it was pretty and it was nice, but he was buying on intrinsic value. He bought and sold. This was quite a considerable outlay for him," he said.

But this wasn't the first stop for this unique treasure. Joe Friedberg had seen this egg first.

According to Friedberg, a man approached him with an offer to be a middleman yet again. This time with a deal for the return of the Third Imperial Easter Egg. And Friedberg did the same thing he had with the Rockwell art. He passed.

Could this Midwestern man

be the same one who approached him about the Rockwell paintings? Another coincidence one can't simply shake off. What are the chances that the Rockwell art, the Fabergé egg, and the ruby slippers would all end up on Friedberg's office doorstep and offered by a seedy character that the lawyer wanted nothing to do with personally? And why would Friedberg finally decide to undertake negotiations when approached by a man about the ruby slippers? What could have made him think this situation would be any different legally than the Rockwell paintings or the Fabergé egg?

Perhaps it was the chance meeting held at a Florida swimming pool in the summer of 2017. It was there where an old friend may have changed his perspective. Something about this latest situation made Friedberg decide that this time it looked different. Maybe he could finally use his influence, and that of his friend, to tighten up those aforementioned frayed ends of this story and bring the case of the missing "traveling pair" of ruby slippers to completion, albeit a muddled one.

PART 2

Chapter 6

The Shoes and the Other Middleman

The following is an exclusive interview with the man responsible, in part, for the return of the "traveling pair" of ruby slippers, Michael R. Insabella, retired United States Secret Service Agent.

Keene: Hello, Mike. Thank you for sitting down and talking to me about the ruby slippers.

Insabella: You're welcome, Jeff.

Keene: Okay, let's jump right into it. Many accounts have identified a "Florida mystery man" or simply the "middleman" as being part of the investigation that led to the recovery of the slippers. Are you that person? Are you the Florida man, the middleman?

Insabella: Yes, I am.

Keene: I understand this may be difficult for you to discuss, considering the circumstances. Why haven't you come forward in the past and identified yourself?

Insabella: There was a time I couldn't. But it's quite easy to talk about now as the fear of being wrongly prosecuted has passed. Having one's reputation thrown to the wind by sloppy policework, however, can overturn your life. I'm almost 75 years old. This has not been easy.

As to why I never came forward until now, well, no one has ever asked me that question until you did. Also, during the latter part of this investigation and recovery, the U.S. attorney in Minneapolis was threatening to prosecute my attorney Joe Friedberg and I for extortion in the negotiations that went on during the recovery of the slippers on behalf of the insurance company, Markel [previously Essex].

Keene: Before we get into the ruby slippers too deeply, let's give the readers some background into your life. I mean, you weren't born a Secret Service agent, right?

Insabella: No, but sometimes it felt that way. I was born and raised in Newark, New Jersey. My father was a boilermaker and my mother was a post office clerk. I was the oldest of three. Ironically, I survived my younger brother and sister. And they left me with lots of nieces and a nephew. I have four children myself, all with kids of their own. I'm a proud grandfather and great-grandfather.

Keene: Where did you attend college? Somewhere in the northeast, I assume.

Insabella: No, actually I graduated from Biscayne College in Miami. Well, now it's St. Thomas of Villanova. That was 1969. But

Antonette "Toni" (Turiano) Insabella, Michael Insabella, and President Gerald Ford, at the White House.

before that, I married my college sweetheart, Antonette Turiano. She went by "Toni." We were married for 30 years until she passed suddenly in 1998. My granddaughter now carries her name. As I said, proud. My first job out of college was patrol officer for the North Miami Beach Police Department. After three years there, I was hired in '71 as a special agent with the Miami Field Office of the Secret Service. From there, 1975 to '80, I was part of the White House detail that protected the presidents.

Keene: Which ones?

Insabella: Ford, Carter, and Reagan. I actually took President Carter's daughter Amy to school as part of my presidential detail responsibilities. My daughters were invited to Amy Carter's birthday parties at the White House.

Keene: I bet you have quite a few pictures.

Insabella: Oh, yeah. A lot of memories. I traveled all over the world and met leaders and dignitaries from many countries. I worked as a special agent in Miami first, then D.C., and finally in the Albuquerque field office where I investigated counterfeit currency cases and worked undercover. I also acted as the chief liaison between the Secret Service and the FBI foreign and domestic terrorism cases, between the Sandia National Labs relating to the Strategic Defense Initiative, and held top secret security clearance with compartmentalized clearance above top secret.

Keene: Impressive. Strategic Defense Initiative? Wasn't that what they called "Star Wars?" That was Reagan's thing, wasn't it?

Insabella: Yes. I received many commendations from those presidents for my service. Once, after completing a joint foreign intelligence terrorism investigation where I worked with the FBI resulting in numerous arrests, I received a letter of commendation from Michael Smelser, the Special Agent in Charge of the Headquarters Foreign Intelligence Branch. He thanked me for my service by writing, "Without exception, his work has been flawless and performed in a very professional manner."

Keene: It sounds like you were very good at your job and really made a difference in the world during a stressful time. I, too, thank you for your service.

Insabella: Thank you. It was hard work, and I was glad that after 23 years I could finally retire to Florida. I felt privileged to work for one of the world's most respected law enforcement agencies, with great colleagues, when the Secret Service was a specialized protective force under the Treasury Department, at an important time in history.

Keene: But you didn't really retire, did you?

Insabella: Not for long. I found out soon enough that my services could be useful in the corporate arena. So, I started my own security consulting firm in '94, MRI Associates. I was hired to do security planning for Presidential inaugurations, among others. A few years later, I became the Director of Executive Protection for Office Depot where I conducted security planning for the chairman, CEO, and other corporate executives.

Keene: That is one colorful background, Mike. You have a solid reputation as a law-abiding patriot. Yet here we are today, conducting this interview over a stain placed upon that reputation by the very agency you worked with as an equal for so many years.

Insabella: It breaks my heart, Jeff. To be accused of something when all the evidence shows otherwise. To have my home be ransacked, my computers and phone confiscated. I'm really still in shock about it all. It has stressed me to the point that I'm physically suffering. I'm no spring chicken.

I was hoping this case would be my investigative swan song. Of course, it would be nice ending my career with the recovery of the slippers. I had hoped it would shed some favorable publicity on the Secret Service at a time when recent publicity has not been flattering.

If this case had been handled properly by the police and FBI, if they had "followed the reward money" with my assistance, not only could they have recovered the slippers but possibly identified the thieves.

38

Keene: I can only imagine. But I think we're getting a little ahead of ourselves with this interview. Let's take a step back. Is that okay? To be clear, we're now talking about the ruby slippers, the ones stolen in 2005, right?

Insabella: Yes, and how I became a pivotal person in their return.

Keene: That's exactly what I'm curious about. From what I understand, the FBI, the Grand Rapids P.D., the entire world would still not have the slippers returned without your help. So, how did you get involved at all in this investigation given your background with the US Secret Service?

Insabella: It all began with a conversation at the swimming pool with my good and old friend Joe Friedberg.

Keene: How did you meet Joe Friedberg?

Insabella: My relationship with Joe Friedberg began in 1999 when I purchased my condo in Florida. Joe was one of the original owners, approximately ten years before I purchased. We became friends, starting out as pool friends. But then realized our families were closely related in age and makeup. And although Joe had come

Michael Insabella, front with hand up, while on presidential detail with Jimmy Carter seen waving behind Insabella.

to Florida maybe two or three times a year, it was mostly during the holidays. So, we spent many a holiday and dinner with Joe and his wife Carolyn. Two of our children actually had the same names and were about the same age. They got along well until they got older, married, and had their own families.

Although Joe was a criminal defense attorney and I a federal agent, we got along fine because we were honest with each other. Joe realized that some of the people he represented were the dregs of the society, the bottom of the barrel, and the most hideous people you could imagine on Earth. He recognized that. But he was of the opinion that they deserved the best defense possible. Win or lose. And in some cases, when he had really bad clients, they pled out. And of course, my history with law enforcement over 34 years, I just wanted to arrest the bad guys and get them off the street for the protection and the good of the public. So, that was my drive, and he understood that. We got along well.

He was a wonderful dinner guest. His wife was smart and witty. And we became good friends over the years and maintain that friendship even today.

Keene: And it was this relationship that made you believe his story about possibly helping recover the stolen slippers?

Insabella: I recognized Joe's prowess and experience as a defense attorney. I know that he had been voted in the top 100 attorneys in the country several times. And he was also considered the patriarch of the criminal defense attorneys in the Minneapolis area. He was a brilliant constitutional attorney and well respected by me and his peers. I had no doubt about the legitimacy of his claim.

CHAPTER 7

SHOES ON THE POOL DECK

In Chapter 5, Joe Friedberg's name arose as a possible source of information regarding the crime syndicate in and around Minneapolis. Considering his substantial work as a defense attorney for 40 years, the FBI put him on the list of interesting characters. Coincidentally, Friedberg and Mike Insabella had been old friends through working in similar fields. They even ended up living in the same condominium complex in Florida. It was there, in the early summer of 2017, where Insabella and Friedberg met while sitting alongside their condo's pool.

Friedberg and Insabella had not been talking about the ruby slippers at all. They conversed about people who Insabella had protected in the past as an agent. Not so much political figures, but celebrities in conjunction with a post-Secret Service job he had taken with the National Italian American Foundation in Washington, D.C.

Before Insabella retired as a Secret Service agent, the National Italian American Foundation would host galas once a year. They were always the largest gathering in Washington, D.C, with around 3,500 sit-down dinner guests. They had a huge celebrity head table consisting of about 60 Italian American personalities, political people, and their supporters.

At one of the events, an accolade was to be presented to Frank Sinatra. During a routine security search of the head table, Sinatra's prize, a Tiffany-designed crystal award, had been accidentally broken into six pieces by one of Insabella's agents. Insabella admitted to the executive director of the National Italian American Foundation, Mr. John Salamone, that Secret Service was responsible. They both went to Frank Sinatra to deliver the bad news. Insabella had known him from previous contacts during the Reagan Administration and asked him personally to not embarrass the Secret Service. He assured Sinatra that he would find a way to replace it even if he had to pay for it himself.

John Salamone was impressed with the way Insabella handled the situation. So much so, that when Insabella retired from service, Salamone asked him to handle security in the future for the galas held each year. Insabella did that job for 13 years. He would hire retired agents in the area and form a security force. When the President attended, he would provide personnel to support the agents who handled security for the President. In that case, Insabella acted as liaison between the foundation and the Secret Service. In times when the President or Vice-President did not attend, he handled the total security for the event focusing on the head table and backstage area which they kept secure. Sometimes, he would also have small protection details on the people being awarded. This included celebrities such as Mohammed Ali for lifetime achievement, Sophia Lauren, and other celebrities and luminaries being recognized.

Continuing with their conversation at the swimming pool, Friedberg asked Insabella who his favorite celebrity was.

He immediately responded. "Joe DiMaggio. I found him to be a dignified, soft-spoken gentleman."

Friedberg then asked who the worst of the details had been.

Insabella responded even faster this time. "Liza Minnelli."

"Why?"

Insabella explained that during one of the galas held at the Hilton Hotel in D.C., Frank Sinatra was being presented posthumously with another award. The honor was to be handed to his

John Salamone and Liza Minnelli at NIAF's 1988 Anniversary Gala.

wife Barbara Sinatra by Liza Minnelli. But during the week, the women apparently had an altercation. Minnelli thought she was being upstaged by Sinatra and was behaving with hostility.

So, on the night of the event of the awards ceremony, Minnelli, obviously intoxicated, became boisterous and obnoxious. At one point, she requested to leave the stage and go back to her room.

John Salamone was more than anxious to have that happen and asked Insabella to escort her up to her room. Exiting through the back doorway by way of the kitchen, they entered a private elevator on the way to the 8th floor. The elevator was manned by a young hotel employee. It wasn't supposed to stop on any of the other floors because it was being manually controlled. But it was apparently programmed to stop at the lobby level regardless of how it was being operated.

The doors slid open and there stood a lady with two young children, maybe seven or eight years old.

Upon seeing them, Minnelli let loose a slurred command. "This is *my* fucking elevator, so find yourself another fucking elevator."

The woman looked at the agents in alarm.

Insabella quickly addressed her. "Security, Ma'am. Please take the next elevator." The agents continued their way up to Minnelli's room. All the while, she remained belligerent and had nothing nice to say about anyone in the hotel or at the National Italian American Foundation.

At the poolside, Friedberg and Insabella laughed about the years old incident.

Friedberg said, "It's funny you mention Liza Minnelli (Judy Garland's daughter) because in the not-too-distant past I had a guy who I represented once before come into my office. He had a woman with him. It was obvious this guy was trying to impress her with how well-connected he was. In his attempt to ingratiate this woman, he told me he knew the people who had the stolen ruby slippers. It seemed to me he was trying to get money out of this woman. I basically tossed him out of my office."

Norman Rockwell paintings. A Fabergé egg. And now Judy Garland's ruby slippers. There seems to be a pattern here.

Insabella responded. "Ruby slippers? What are you talking about?"

Friedberg then relayed the story to him about how the slippers had been stolen from a museum in Grand Rapids, Minnesota. Then he said, "You know, I think there's a reward of a million dollars being offered."

This was the pivotal moment when Friedberg approached Insabella with information that could possibly lead to the return of the ruby slippers. He asked for Insabella's assistance due to his extensive background in law enforcement. Insabella agreed. Both were certain with his exemplary credentials he could easily coordinate with the FBI to ensure the slippers were returned

safely and properly authenticated. And a reward would be a nice bonus for their efforts.

The reward Friedberg mentioned was one offered anonymously by a private citizen after the shoes had gone missing and after Michael Shaw had already received his insurance payout. According to John Miner, a Judy Garland Museum board member, that citizen was in Arizona and a *Wizard of Oz* mega-fan. In 2015, at the ten-year anniversary of the theft, that zealous person posted a $1 million bounty for credible information leading to their return.

Insabella said, "Well, that's interesting. I'll reach out and see if I still have any contacts with the Minnelli camp. I'll do that through John Salamone."

Insabella called Salamone and asked if he still had contacts. He wasn't sure, given that it had been several years. But he said he'd reach out. He called back the next day and told Insabella he no longer had the contacts. "They've dried up. However, there's a ton of information about the ruby slippers online. If you want to find out more, you can read what's on there, and you'll be fully briefed on the origin of the slippers, as well as the theft."

After reading what was posted on the internet, Insabella contacted John Kelsch, director of the Judy Garland Museum, and sent him a copy of his résumé, including his contact numbers and home address. Kelsch referred him to Ms. Jean Gardner of the Merkel Insurance Company. He told Insabella that Essex (the original insurance company) had paid a claim in the amount of $800,000 to Michael Shaw, the owner of the slippers, and that Essex had a confidentiality agreement with Shaw in the event the slippers were recovered.

On July 5th, 2017, Insabella was advised the existing reward was for only $200,000—and that it was about to be withdrawn.

CHAPTER 8

THE BIG SHOE SALE

In Insabella's initial correspondence to John Kelsch, he had written, "At this time, I cannot verify the lead I spoke to you about. I can, however, vouch for the source as being reliable in the past. Please, let's keep this within a close group."

The next day, Kelsch replied, "I received the résumé. What is the next step?"

Insabella needed to know who the owners were. "My informant

John Kelsch

and the holder have different motivations for moving forward. Money is a consideration of both. We need a contract that will establish the transfer of the reward and keep the informant confidential."

Kelsch replied simply with, "I will get to work on this."

A week passed.

Insabella followed up with an email. "Any more for me on this case?"

Kelsch answered the next day. "Essex Insurance owns the slippers. However, a confidentiality agreement exists between Michael Shaw and the insurance company should they be recovered."

"Where do I go next? Can you introduce me to Essex's attorney?" Insabella knew how to move an investigation forward.

Kelsch provided the name of Jean Gardner. When Insabella contacted her, a series of protracted negotiations ensued between the "holder of the shoes," who Friedberg was in contact with through an intermediary, and the insurance company, Markel, who now owned the shoes, wherever they were. Insabella acted as a middleman, a negotiator for the safe return of a treasured piece of Americana. It is reminiscent of how the fictional character Indiana Jones would often refer to one of his unique and historical finds when he said, "It belongs in a museum." Insabella was of the same motivation.

On June 23, 2017, Insabella telephoned Gardner. "I was told by John Kelsch to contact you regarding the return of the ruby slippers. My information comes from a reliable but confidential informant who has provided very sensitive information in the past."

Five days went by.

Insabella followed up with an email to Gardner. "I believe that my lead may be time sensitive."

Another week. Still no reply.

Insabella reached out again. "Was there any interest in following up on my lead?"

Gardner finally replied via email. "There is an existing reward of $200,000 from ten years ago that their client would still agree to follow, subject to all its terms. The reward will be withdrawn shortly. So, if there is any intention to take action, it must happen quickly. We require proof that the slippers are real."

Insabella returned with a multi-part proposal. The criteria established to determine how the slippers can be authenticated, the written contract specifying "reward to me as agent, by your client, upon return of the slippers, the reward money is to be put in an attorney's trust account and mutually accepted, the slippers are to be delivered to the attorney's office, and finally, once the slippers are authenticated, the reward money is to be released."

As it turned out, Insabella's efforts were hampered by both sides' intractable behavior. The terms of the deal—the amount of the reward, how to authenticate the shoes, who would pay for the authentication, and who would go first—were all up for argument. Neither the insurance company nor the anonymous holders of the ruby slippers could agree on something so simple as would the shoes be produced first or would the reward be paid first. As a middleman, neither in possession of the shoes nor controlling the reward, Insabella's hands were tied. His efforts as an intermediary served simply as a conduit of information between those who had the shoes and the insurance company. He did not anticipate either side would be so demanding as to the terms of the deal.

In a further interview with Michael Insabella, he stated, "The chain of custody had multiple links. As a result, to this day I have no knowledge of who stole the slippers or who possessed them at any point in time. At no time during the negotiation did I have direct communication with anyone claiming to possess the slippers, and I never possessed them myself."

The insurance company had initially offered $200,000 for return of the slippers. This made sense since they were originally covered for one million dollars, and Michael Shaw was already paid 80% of that. However, the "holder of the shoes" turned down this offer. They were aware of the million-dollar reward offered by the anonymous Arizona devotee and wanted more.

Was this "holder of the shoes" the original thief? Was there any tie to actor Louie Anderson's now deceased brother?[2] Maybe the holder was simply a storage facility employee who found the slippers in some southern California abandoned repository who realized what he'd found and tried to earn a promised reward legally. These were questions with no answers.

On January 21, 2022, it was announced that Louie Anderson died in Las Vegas from complications of large B-cell lymphoma at the age of 68.

Death has historically proven to be a convenient way to hide the truth—a truth already disarrayed by 13 years of both criminal obscurity and media sensationalism. Rumors buried beneath rumors.

Throughout this series of negotiations, Insabella kept Attorney Joe Friedberg updated. Then Friedberg dropped a bomb.

In an email to only Insabella with the subject "Memorializing attorney-client relationship," Friedberg stated, "As I understand the matter, these shoes are in the possession of an unknown individual who has determined to destroy them if he or she cannot participate in a lawful return of the property pursuant to the posted award." He then suggested that Insabella contact the Grand Rapids Police Department.

"Will do. I don't really trust Jean [Gardner]."

In continuation with the interview from Chapter 6, Insabella had this to say about his initial communication with the police:

"Ms. Gardner advised me that Detective Brian Mattson was handling the case for the Grand Rapids P.D. and return of any slippers would have to be coordinated through him. I had numerous conversations and forwarded emails exchanged between me and Detective Mattson. During the initial contact with Mattson, I identified my source for the information as an informant. The informant was, in fact, Joe Friedberg. Joe had asked me initially to remain anonymous during any contacts with the insurance company or the police department. I took this to mean that the information he was going to provide to me was probably privileged and that the holders of the slippers were possibly clients of his or friends of clients of his. This was very important for me to maintain because I know that Joe Friedberg had represented many dangerous clients over the years, including organized crime figures. The thought that any information provided to him by his clients had been leaked by him to law enforcement might have put his life at danger. So, I respected that and referred to him initially as my informant, not as my friend Joe Friedberg or subsequently my attorney Joe Friedberg."

Friedberg reassured Insabella. "Tony Markel, founder and former CEO [of the insurance company], is an old friend."

Insabella took his colleague's advice and on July 11th sent his résumé to Detective Brian Mattson of the Grand Rapids P.D.

Mattson was originally a narcotics detective. When he was handed down the case of the ruby slippers, it had been plagued by a decade of dead ends. Any evidence was dated and virtually useless. For example, the crime scene photos were stored on a floppy disk. Mattson was often tormented with bad and often humorous leads.

A woman was arrested and held in the Itasca County jail on unrelated charges. She said she had information regarding the ruby slippers. "Two guys, from the drug world, broke into the museum and stole the slippers. I wore them just the other day. They're in a green shoebox. But the guys didn't know what to do with them so they were going to throw them in the Buckeye Pit."

She then provided them with the location of the men's trailer. Since the local quarry pits had already been searched by divers, this was the only new place to search. When the officers arrived, they found the home hidden deep in the woods surrounded by outbuildings. The people living there were obviously hoarders.

Mattson knocked on the door around sunset.

A man answered. "Sure, I've got them."

After searching through a multitude of boxes, they found a green box in a cluttered closet. Inside were a pair of ruby shoes.

Clearly inscribed on the shoes was the evidence Mattson needed. "Made in China."

"I bought those at a garage sale." Disappointment spread across his face. "I thought I bought a gold mine."

They were fakes. Mattson later referred to them as "stripper shoes." Another dead end.

Finally, in July of 2017, he received a phone call from Insabella.

On July 13th, Mattson wrote in an email to Insabella, "I have been in touch with several entities to confirm the continued existence of the reward monies. This is being validated. But the manner in which the reward money is released will have to be worked out." He then told Insabella that he had a local attorney on board to facilitate the process and that he was working out validation with Essex Insurance. He wanted to keep their dealings "as quiet as possible and not draw any attention that would hamper the transaction from coming to fruition." He then reassured Insabella that he has "so far been able to keep his identity confidential."

Four days later, Mattson wrote, "The insurance company is agreeable to a contract regarding the payout of reward for return of the slippers, and one is being drafted."

Insabella then forwarded that message to Joe Friedberg along with information from a 2006 appraisal of the slippers with a detailed description. He then responded to Mattson. "We await the contract from the owner/insurer and the details of the authentication process." Mattson told him the authentication meeting would take place on July 20th.

These messages go back and forth between Friedberg on one end and Mattson and the insurance company on the other. All the while, Insabella played the negotiator. Imagine being a referee in a football game where you are being told exactly what to do by the coach of each team but they can't agree on any of the logistics so the conversation keeps going back and forth, the clock is ticking down, and nothing is moving anywhere. Referees have the power to act. Insabella had none.

Insabella continued:

"I reported the proposed logistics to my informant [Joe Friedberg in Minnesota]. He ran the logistics down the ladder to the holders of the slippers. They offered to negotiate for the amount of the reward but rejected any police involvement. I reported back to Detective Mattson and Jean Gardner. I proposed a compromised solution which would include demands from both sides. On July 17th, Detective Mattson reported that Essex Insurance, now Markel, was agreeable to the terms and would draft a contract. On July 24th, Detective Mattson reported, and apologized, that "no contract from Markel would be coming."

Hours of hard work and communications were getting nothing done. The stress took its toll. All Insabella wanted was to return a stolen property of cultural significance. He was attempting to provide an important public service that his background and expertise working undercover made him uniquely qualified to perform. Without his assistance, Judy Garland's ruby slippers might be destroyed by the holders if they felt threatened.

He had to press on.

Jean Gardner, the insurance company representative, finally contacted Insabella on July 28th. She ensured the deal would go through but they needed "some good faith effort." She insisted on seeing photographic evidence and for Insabella's "word that it is a valid picture of what is being held by the party."

Insabella responded in kind and got to work on obtaining photos of the slippers, wherever they were. He then contacted Friedberg.

In the meantime, Gardner grew impatient.

Insabella explained via email. "The delay is because I do not have possession of the slippers and must reach out to my contact who has to reach out to his contact to get anything done. I have no problem working with Detective Mattson, and that has not set well with the holder of the slippers. There is a good chance this deal will go south and for the slippers to go into hiding for another ten years. The holder does not seem to be concerned with your deadline [of August

15th] for the reward. It has been suggested that the slippers could be sold elsewhere. They still have questions about the amount of the reward. We'll know more when and if the photos are produced."

Finally, eleven days later, on August 12th, Insabella received the photos from Friedberg via the U.S Postal Service and immediately forwarded them via email to the insurance company, care of Jean Gardner. He had laid the glossy photos out on his dining room table and used his personal cell phone to record the images. The brown wood of the furniture was plainly visible in the background of these photographs of photos.

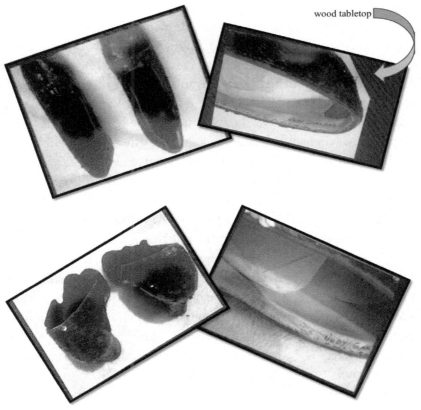

Michael Insabella took these photos of the received photographs with his cell phone in his dining room. 1-top view of both shoes, 2 - "Judy Garland" can be seen along the shoe's inner edge, 3 - rear view of the shoes, 4 - inside the other shoe.

He then attached them to the email and informed Gardner he would be taking a vacation out of the country with his new wife Marion for six weeks in September. This had dragged on long enough. Far longer than necessary. Insabella knew this wasn't a matter of life and death. The shoes could wait. He needed a break.

Little did Insabella know, Mattson had gleaned the geotag information from the pictures he had taken and was now privy to his location. His private home in Jensen Beach, Florida. Well, that's Mattson's story. The truth is that he already had Insabella's contact information via the résumé. It started to seem like someone wanted more than just to get the slippers back.

But Insabella did not pilfer the shoes nor was he ever in possession of them. In a letter dated August 17th, Dave Washburn, a claims director with Markel Service, Incorporated, agreed "that if the slippers are returned to the Grand Rapid [sic] Police Department by Michael Insabella by August 30, 2017 and subsequently authenticated," "the reward payment, less the fees and costs" "will be issued to Michael Insabella, provided no other party claims right to the reward." Additionally, in a letter dated August 28th, Scott Johnson, Chief of Police of the Grand Rapids Police Department, stated, "The Minnesota statute of limitations for the offense of burglary has expired. It is not possible to bring criminal charges against the person(s) who committed this act for the offense of burglary. If the shoes are delivered to the Grand Rapids Police Department and an explanation provided as to how this crime took place and where the slippers have been over the past 12 years then the Grand Rapids Police Department has no interest in presenting a criminal investigation to a prosecutor asking for charging review for the offense of burglary, possession of stolen property or any other crime, at the state or federal level. We will not do so."

The letter went on to state, "The Grand Rapids Police Department's sole concern now is to recover this piece of historical memorabilia so that the insurance company can be made whole and make these shoes again available for the public to view and appreciate."

At that point, it seemed to everyone that Insabella, the insurance company, and the police department were all in agreement.

On August 28th, Mattson sent this email to Insabella. "The Chief of Police and the city attorney are drafting letters indicating they have no interest in prosecution on the state or federal level." Apparently, the statute of limitations had run out, as well.

Finally, on August 29th, Insabella received a letter from John Dimich, the Grand Rapids City Prosecutor. The letter echoed the police department's communication and added, "As the City's prosecutor, I will not issue any criminal charges related to the disappearance of the slippers or their return to the Grand Rapids Police Department."

At this time, the insurance company's deadline of August 30th was fast approaching and "the holders" were still not satisfied with the reward amount. Nor did they want the police involved at all. Gardner grew impatient again. She wrote, "Where do we stand? The experts want to know if the slippers are coming."

Insabella told her he was still waiting on his attorney, who had a trial all week, to go over the Chief of Police's letter regarding their having no interest in prosecution. On August 29th, Insabella revealed to Gardner and Mattson that Friedberg is indeed his attorney and that his advice to Insabella is "for me to stay out of any further negotiations as they pertain to reward money and logistics." He then informed them that he "will continue to pass information to "the holder" and will wait for you to propose solutions to the problems raised by "the holder." Joe [Friedberg] will represent me in my absence and in all future involvement in the case."

That same day, the letter from the Grand Rapids City Prosecutor arrived stating there would be no prosecution on their part. But there was a problem. Friedberg informed Insabella it was the County of Itasca who would have jurisdiction over felonies, not the city attorney. He also made note that there was no mention of the federal government in the statement. Too many loopholes. It would seem the safety net for The Middleman and his attorney was questionable.

The insurance company's deadline had arrived. And it looked like the negotiations would have to start all over again at this point. On August 31st, Mattson sent an email reaffirming the letters from the Chief of Police and the city attorney. He added, "At this point, the goal is to see the ruby slippers returned, and to hear a story of their journey since they were stolen in August 2005." It appeared as if Mattson was baiting Insabella.

And it was here where the talks stalled.

CHAPTER 9

GUMSHOES

Six weeks went by with no communication from either the insurance company or the "holder of the shoes." As far as Michael Insabella was concerned, the deal was now off. He had spent September 10 to October 5, 2017 visiting Portugal's Azores Islands, and the last thing on his mind was Judy Garland's famous footwear.

In an interview with a reporter, Mattson stated that he thought the shoes might have been traveling with Insabella, so he called his friend in the FBI for help. Chris Dudley answered the phone, and Mattson asked him to join the case. He wasn't getting anywhere and feared the case was taking a downward spiral.

For the first part of the phone call, Dudley thought Mattson was crazy. Twenty minutes went by where Mattson explained everything about the case he could. Dudley eventually put the call on speaker. In a matter of 45 minutes, people from the office had crowded around Dudley's desk saying things like, "We can't wait to get started."

Mattson had accomplished what private investigator Rob Feeney could not, securing the involvement of the FBI. And although Feeney met with Mattson to help identify the slippers from Insabella's photos, the authorities never provided him with the full information regarding the case. He still thinks Insabella was the thief requesting the reward money.

Life took hold of Insabella's plans once more. Earlier that year, his doctors discovered a nearly complete blockage of his carotid artery. The blockage was life-threatening, so he underwent surgery to correct the problem.

In September, Insabella married Marion Calbough in the Azores. But in October, after his return, the doctors found additional blockages in Insabella's heart. He endured more surgery, this time open-heart, bypassing two arteries. He was out of commission from then until December 2017. During this time, Friedberg handled all communication and logistics with Markel and the police regarding the return of the slippers and payment of any reward.

On November 9th, the insurance company contacted Insabella and asked to reopen the negotiations. "There is still some interest in seeing whether the slippers can be recovered." They hadn't given up. Who would? "We haven't spoken since August. Are the slippers still around? Is there any interest in continuing discussions on their return?" Insabella and Friedberg agreed to continue with their efforts. Even with Insabella's condition, he still partook in the negotiations to return the slippers.

After another month of back-and-forth emails requesting better photos, more money, and more time, Friedberg wrote to Gardner. "My information is the holders are a bit cranky and say the photos you have are the best they can do." He proposed they agree on a number and arrange to send one of the shoes. Once that shoe was authenticated, they will send the other upon release of the escrow. "I have no authority for this proposal. I am trying to be creative without consulting with what I believe to be inordinately peculiar clients."

Four more months went by and nothing more occurred than the same vacillating exchanges. Then, in April 2018, news of a new Judy Garland movie starring Renée Zellweger was released. The value of the slippers was now estimated to exceed $6 million. "The holders" saw dollar signs. Insabella had to let Gardner know. "The holder's price went up. They want $500,000. My fear is that if our communication breaks down with the holder, another avenue for selling the slippers may be sought. It smells like the deal may be going south."

During this time, Detective Mattson and Agent Dudley were hatching a plan to get the shoes regardless of monetary promises. Mattson has since stated, "I was not trying to put anyone in handcuffs or turn this into a criminal case. I just wanted the slippers back." So, it didn't matter what "the holders" and the insurance company agreed upon. Their plan was to sweeten the deal and lure in those shoes as quick and dirty as possible. The insurance company was in on it too, damn the innocent.

After nearly a year of negotiation, the insurance company promised to pay $400,000 if the shoes were returned safely. "The holder" finally agreed. In an email at the conclusion of the negotiations, the insurance company wrote, "Both parties have entered this transaction in good faith and I'd like to complete it in the same manner."

From May 14 through June 4, 2018, Insabella and his new wife traveled again to the Azores for a religious feast. He had advised Gardner that he heard the slippers would be sent to Friedberg and that Friedberg needed a signed contract to handle the authentication and delivery. From that point on, all contact with Markel was handled by Friedberg. The exchange was set for July 10th in Minneapolis.

An email from Gardner dated July 3rd states, "I'm excited that this might finally work out for everyone. I may actually retire if this closes one of my favorite claims." Another email from Gardner dated July 6th states, "Mike, for years I have told everyone that if I am ever successful in getting the slippers back, I am retiring on that high note. I'm counting on you to make this happen so I can retire! The beach calls." Gardner then promised other insurance agents would be present for the transaction. "Val and Dave are great people and you will enjoy hanging out with them while the slippers are reviewed by the expert that they got. You can tell them Tony Markel stories."

On July 5, 2018, Friedberg informed Gardner he would meet at the time and place of her choosing. "The shoes will be delivered within a few minutes of our meeting. Then we can get some coffee."

Gardner replied with, "We'll need to take a raincheck on that coffee."

Throughout these negotiations, Michael Insabella worked alongside Joe Friedberg. The criminal defense attorney's advice and assistance served to bring the negotiations to fruition. Once the deal was struck, Friedberg arranged to take custody of the ruby slippers and deliver them to Circa Gallery, an art gallery in Minneapolis, where they could be authenticated. An expert confirmed the shoes were the actual missing pair. His next stop was a coffee shop, the designated location for the exchange. There, he met with a man who claimed to be the insurance company representative and was presented with a $400,000 check, as agreed.

But it wasn't an insurance company representative. It turns out, Gardner was working with the FBI to build Insabella's and Friedberg's trust.

Before Friedberg could depart, several FBI agents appeared and confiscated the check and the shoes. It was a sting operation. The insurance company kept the money and the ruby slippers.

At the same instant, 10 AM to be precise, about twenty FBI agents, many heavily armed, entered and swarmed Insabella's home in Florida. They had a search warrant. But Insabella stated they didn't need one, as he readily cooperated, inviting the agents into his home voluntarily. They searched in vain for the slippers. But they were also ordered to seize computers, phones, and any data associated with the missing shoes. Insabella could not give them what he did not have. And he had no information they didn't already know.

Accompanying the agents were support officers from two local police departments, a search team, a photographer, an inventory specialist, and an interview team. Even with all his experience, Insabella and his wife were shocked.

They had only moved into their new home the week before the

FBI came to the door. Insabella had just convinced his wife to downsize. She agreed, reluctantly.

Understandably, their neighbors were frightened by the extreme show of force. Insabella later said, "The vibe here will never be the same."

Insabella continually assured his wife to not worry. He had done nothing wrong. He told her they had a search warrant and were required to search the residence. He showed the agents over 100 emails associated with the case. He presented the photographs he had sent to Detective Mattson and Jean Gardner. But it was clear the Florida FBI did not know the slippers had been delivered ten minutes earlier in Minneapolis. They had been told by someone that the slippers were in Florida and when the holders had demanded more money from Markel, it was considered an extortion attempt.

Several times during the search of Insabella's home, the lead agent was seen stepping outside to speak to the agent in Minnesota who was in the process of recovering the slippers from Friedberg. Although the conversation could not be heard, Insabella attests it was a very animated discussion and the local agent repeatedly shook his head "no."

When the agent reentered, Insabella explained he was only a conduit in this case and acting in good faith. He told him, "I was acting as an agent on behalf of the insurance company. At most, I expected a 10% finder's fee from any reward plus expenses, but the bulk of the reward was to go to my informant who would disperse it by letting it trickle down the ladder to the holders." During the interview, many of the logistical nuisances were discussed.

The agents were not allowed to show Insabella the affidavit of the search warrant from the interview questions. He determined that Markel or the Grand Rapids Police Department had sought the FBIs involvement in this case. Only by reporting to them that the ruby slippers were in Florida at his house would they be able to make this an interstate case within the FBI's jurisdiction with statutory authority to investigate.

When Insabella suggested this to the agents, they appeared as if they had been misled. But by who?

Later, the FBI agents were quoted as saying, "They fell for it. Was the plan that convincing, or were the contacts that bad at committing crimes?"

Had Insabella and Friedberg committed a crime? According to the government, since the middleman and his attorney negotiated for more than the $200,000 reward that the insurance company originally offered, some say they *had* taken part in extortion.

On the same day, Insabella received an email at 1:52 PM from Friedberg:

"As you probably know at this time the transaction was completed and the FBI seized the check. Their theory is that at 200,000 it was a legal transaction and at 400,000 it was 200 worth of extortion. I told them they were completely wrong. They also wanted me to think that they thought you might have been the possessor of the shoes and told them that was ridiculous. They don't really think so. We should talk and I will be glad to refer you to a lawyer that I know quite well who won't charge you anything at this stage.

"They also wanted me to identify others and I said I would not. The fact that I would be unable to was not discussed.

"Remember, I not only have another lawyer's opinion on this but as a tax criminal lawyer as well and my own research wherein I advised you that this transaction was completely legal for you and me. Since we didn't do anything wrong and in fact provided a public service you can call me.

"Joe"

Which was it? Did they commit extortion or not? It was time to find a lawyer who was not involved in the case.

CHAPTER 10

THE SHOES STRIKE AGAIN

Michael Insabella and his friend Joe Friedberg would never see a dime of any reward money.

At this point in the story, the "traveling pair" of ruby slippers had caused some major disruptions in people's lives, beginning with the tragic tale of Judy Garland's substance abuse and downfall to the succeeding men and women who coveted them. Were Insabella and Friedberg made to suffer as well for their involvement? Were they working for the good of the many or for their own personal gain?

Insabella's new attorney, Robert Richman, has been unable to persuade the prosecutors that he did not act with intent to extort anyone. He attests that he has spent his career honorably serving his country as a Secret Service agent. He has protected presidents, celebrities, dignitaries, and business executives. He spent decades in law enforcement and always comported himself with the highest ethical standards. He begs the question, "Would I throw all that out the window, blinded by greed?"

Richman's law office generated a letter on August 29, 2018, shortly after the FBI's raid on Insabella's home. In it, he defines extortion:

"A person acting with an "intent to extort," as required by 18 U.S.C. § 875(d), or by "wrongful use of . . . fear," as required by the Hobbs Act, 18 U.S.C. § 1951, does not do so openly, as Mr.

Insabella did. Mr. Insabella made no secret of his identity, even supplying his home address to Ms. Gardner when requested. An extortionist does not contact the police to participate in the negotiations. He does not consult with counsel. He does not accept payment by check, for deposit in a trust, set up by his attorney. Mr. Insabella did all of those things."

Michael Insabella never attempted to conceal his identity. He never had the power to effectuate any threat, but merely communicated the information he was provided. With that logic in mind, if one were to be found guilty of such behavior, then every hostage negotiator should be arrested for the crimes of the hostage takers. Even if Markel, the insurance company, had demanded the slippers be returned, Insabella had no way of accomplishing that feat. Moreover, here Markel had already offered a reward and made clear it was open to negotiation as to the amount. To suggest, in those circumstances, that taking Markel up on its offer was a crime, is absurd.

Yet, four years later, the FBI still holds Insabella's personal property and has made no effort to remove the tarnish on his, until now, spotless reputation.

Agent Michael Insabella (back, left) while on protection detail for
President and Mrs. Reagan.

To understand why, let's look at how the FBI handled themselves after the fact.

"I'm surprised they took the bait."

"I'm surprised it worked."

"The insurance company had to play a part, and everyone did a top-notch performance."

"Everyone did their job flawlessly."

What were the FBI agents talking about here? They are celebrating their victory over what they perceived was a criminal act. They saw Insabella and Friedberg as 'people helping criminals' rather than 'people helping the citizens of America by returning the most expensive and cherished piece of Hollywood memorabilia in history.'

During an interview, an FBI agent theorized as to Insabella and Friedberg's involvement. "I'm going to guess that they were successful in other endeavors like this. So, you do what you are comfortable with. What you know. And it if works, they just roll with it."

The agent assumed that Insabella, regardless of his honorable past, commonly extorts insurance companies. This author hasn't checked, but is it common for Secret Service agents to retire into a life of crime? And is it common for agents of the Federal Bureau of Investigation to slander innocent retired civil servants during interviews?

On the day of the seizures, a large number of agents positioned themselves around the coffee shop in Minneapolis for the sting. The FBI had eyes on Friedberg the moment he arrived in town and they tailed him. He had the bag containing the shoes. At one point, Friedberg placed the bag on the counter and went into the bathroom.

Two FBI agents entered, one disguised as the agreed upon insurance agent and the other as the artifact authenticator. Once they met Friedberg, other agents entered, seized everything, and detained Friedberg for questioning. They grilled him for hours while other agents stormed Insabella's Florida condominium frightening his wife and neighbors.

Detective Mattson told an investigative reporter, "The lawyer spilled the beans [to the agents]. He even told them who stole the shoes. Almost off the bat." But the only name he divulged was Kent Anderson, Louie Anderson's deceased brother. The FBI had no power to arrest Friedberg so they released him.

Outside, Friedberg spotted Mattson from across the street. He approached Mattson and said, "You probably want to get a good lawyer."

After seizing the shoes, the FBI continued to flaunt their perceived victory over criminals they never met nor took into custody. Their prize was the famed ruby slippers. And the ill-fated shoes made those agents' boastfulness clear to all.

Agents from the FBI Art Crime Team were tasked with bringing the ruby slippers onto an airplane bound for Washington, D.C. and the Smithsonian. It was their goal to have the shoes authenticated by comparing them to the only other pair known to be in a secure government facility. And there were experts there to confirm it. On the flight, an attendant asked the agents if they wanted to put the box in the overhead luggage rack. They explained that they had purchased a seat for the box. Her curiosity piqued.

Upon arrival, Dawn Wallace, Objects Conservator at the National Museum of American History, received the "traveling pair" while agents hovered about. Wallace had spent time working on the "people's pair," so it was only logical for her to be the one to examine the recovered set. Wallace easily confirmed their authenticity.

They were made the same. However, a bead and some threading differed. No one knew this as they were probably due to repairs made on the movie set while filming. Ryan Lintelman was the curator of the ruby slipper display. He was called in to verify Wallace's conclusions.

In the Conservation Lab, clues revealed that the slippers had been cared for during their 13-year hiatus. However, the inscription bearing Judy Garland's name appeared to have been partially rubbed off, and there was a layer of dirt on them. So, it seemed the shoes had been kept out of sight but certainly not placed in a museum where professionals could care for them. One interesting mystery had been solved upon the reunion of the two pairs. It had been known for years that the pair the Smithsonian housed was a mismatched pair. It just so happened that the stolen pair was the matching left and right shoes! This was the final piece that confirmed the ruby slippers' authenticity.

Lintelman took note afterwards of how the FBI agents placed their badges on the table next to the shoes and took pictures. They wanted the recognition for having found the slippers. To Hell with Michael Insabella and Joe Friedberg who put their reputations and possibly their lives on the line in returning the shoes while FBI agents with little to no effort took all the credit.

The Minneapolis press conference that let the world know the shoes were found proved no different. It was a media circus where the FBI took all the credit. But the pageantry did not sit well with everyone. Particularly Insabella and Friedberg. Even the curator for the Judy Garland Museum in Grand Rapids scoffed at the ridiculous event knowing the officers of Grand Rapids were in over their heads from the beginning.

Rob Feeney, in addition to being a private investigator, is also a movie prop collector and reseller in Minneapolis who also works in the legal realm. He was interviewed in October 2018 by Brooks Johnson of the Forum News Service. Feeney said, "Last year, but more so during the live press conference, all of a sudden it's the FBI everything, and that led me to wonder what's going on there. It's not about who gets credit, it's about the honest truth of it." Feeney felt the FBI not sharing credit, particularly for his part in the recovery, was deceitful.

Jill Sanborn, Special Agent in charge of the Minneapolis division of the FBI, was the spokesperson at the press conference.

She butchered the famous line from the movie as she removed the velvet cloth from atop the plexiglass case by stating, "And now, *Under the Rainbow*." And all the cameras were there to record the swelled heads of the agents.

In November 2018, Scott Johnson, Grand Rapids Police Chief, said, "You see, law enforcement and case investigation is never about grand standing and egos. It is about working together within an agency and as partners between agencies to solve crimes. Who should get credit for recovering the Ruby Red Slippers? Who cares?"

Retired Special Agent Michael Insabella agrees. His only concern is clearing his name from any wrongdoing. That should be everyone else's concern as well.

It appears as if the desire for recognition and some fleeting time in the spotlight brought out the curse once more and made those who revel in receiving false credit appear foolish to the rest of the world.

CHAPTER 11

TYING UP LOOSE SHOESTRINGS

I contacted Michael Insabella for a follow-up interview once again before closing this chapter of infamous American Hollywood history.

Keene: Mike, do you have any hostility toward the FBI regarding the way they conducted themselves in this matter with the ruby slippers?

Insabella: I consider the FBI to be the premier investigating agency, not only in this country, but in the world. They have the resources, and the manpower, and the expertise to handle just about any type of investigation.

Although I have been referred to as the Florida mystery man, the FBI, the Grand Rapids P.D., and the insurance company knew my identity, my address, and all my contact information from the start. Although I requested anonymity at first, and especially anonymity for my informant, this anonymity was certainly broken and trumped when the FBI searched my home. I see no reason why these agencies would not give my name to the media or to other agencies unless there was something that they didn't want me to tell you.

Keene: I'm searching for the right question here. Are you holding on to a secret, Mike?

Insabella: Nothing as serious as a secret. Just an . . . observation, really. One based upon my many years of experience in the Secret Service. You see, the FBI gets into trouble when their investigations are politically motivated or there's a high-profile case with other agencies involved. The FBI has had the reputation of taking over cases with publicity attached that will enhance their image. In many cases, this means taking cases away from local and state police agencies who initiate the case and investigate the leads. I think this was one of those scenarios.

Of course, when the FBI gets involved in political cases, their image is enhanced or suffers depending on which side they choose.

Keene: It seems as if you are agreeing with Hollywood's depiction of that agency. I can recall many movies where that situation is incorporated into the story.

Insabella: During my time in Washington, D.C., I was the Secret Service liaison to the Washington Field office of the FBI. I worked with several agents in the counter-terrorism section. They were among the finest agents I've ever worked with and most hardworking. The problem with these high-profile cases, and this is what Hollywood has fun dramatizing, is that many times they get out of the hands of the local agent working on the case, the guy on the street. Once they're managed by headquarters . . . Well, when that happens, image and publicity is all important. And sometimes the cases take the course I feel this case has taken.

Keene: To be clear, you are saying that someone in the agency, or maybe even the insurance company for the slippers, lied? Is that the "secret?" Let me rephrase that. Is that the observation you've made?

Insabella: If I could see the affidavit for the search warrant that was filed in West Palm Beach, and signed by a local magistrate, —by the way, this document, this affidavit, has been sealed by the court—I will know exactly who lied, embellished, or misrepresented the facts of this case. The facts are that, very innocently, I got involved in a case which could have led to a respected piece of Hollywood memorabilia being returned to the public and to the rightful owners. The money aspect of this case is non-existent.

The finder's fee that was expected of me wouldn't even cover my expenses in this case, let alone my time.

Keene: Now that the slippers have been recovered, certainly thanks in part to you, what would you like to see happen with them?

Insabella: My hope is that for the future these slippers be returned not to some rich guy, not to some insurance company, but to a place where they can be viewed by the public. To me, that place would be the Smithsonian Institute in Washington, D.C. Perhaps, some consideration can be given to the Judy Garland Museum in Grand Rapids so they could be exhibited there for part of the year.

I have no skin in what happens to the slippers in the future. I have counted any money due me as a loss, and I feel at my age and medical condition that pursuing any lawsuit against Markel, even though probably appropriate, is just not in my best interests.

So, that's how I'm viewing this in the future. Others might feel differently. If the FBI or the U.S. attorney in Minnesota feels that they can support a criminal case against me, let them bring it on.

Keene: But didn't they take everything? What evidence do you have?

Insabella: It's true, that during the FBI search, items were taken

Agent Michael Insabella (4th from the left) receiving an award from the FBI at FBI Headquarter in Washington, D.C.

from my house. Items said to be returned within two weeks. There were three laptop computers, one that had recently been taken off my boat, my wife's laptop, and my laptop, along with miscellaneous office supplies.

But most importantly, about twenty flash drives had been taken and retained. These flash drives contained business information from my consulting work as well as my job as Director of Executive Protection for Office Depot. They included all my contacts abroad as well as my contacts locally for doing my work. The things I need for my job. Contacts for car rental business, flight information, hotels, and personnel used in conducting business. These were taken and not given back to me.

What I do still have are copies of all the emails sent between Jean Gardner, myself, and Detective Mattson. I would invite you to take copies of these emails and draw whatever conclusions you feel are appropriate for your investigation.

Keene: Thank you for your openness. With all this being said, and how you were treated many ways by all involved, including the FBI, if the slippers were to be returned to the Smithsonian Institute in Washington, D.C., would you visit them?

Insabella: Not a chance.

Keene: Why not?

Insabella: I've chalked my efforts and time spent on the ruby slippers as a loss. It's a closed case.

That it is.

CHAPTER 12

A MILE IN SOMEONE ELSE'S SHOES

The tragedy of the ruby slippers has been described in the pages of this book. And it may be difficult for an outsider to understand how an inanimate object could be the cause of all these events. There is another sample of evidence yet to share.

American actress and singer Frances Ethel Gumm, better known to the world as Judy Garland, died of an accidental barbiturate overdose at the age of 47 on Sunday, June 22, 1969. The ruby slippers were found only a few months later in the spring of 1970 by "Hollywood Robinhood" Kent Warner.

Emma Bull, an American science fiction and fantasy author, is quoted as saying, "Coincidence is the word we use when we can't see the levers and pulleys." The Wizard of Oz, from behind the shiny green curtains, pulled his levers and used pulleys to convince others of his power. Is the coincidence of Garland's passing and immediate finding of her shoes the universe just pulling strings? Or is something more sinister at play?

Are you thinking what I'm thinking? What if the dark spirit that tormented and abused Garland all her years found its way to the shoes as they lay dormant in that abandoned backlot loft? What other object, full of movie magic or otherwise, could have been chosen that bound Garland so tightly to the roots of her tragic life?

Just imagine that ethereal essence rising from Cadogan Lane

Judy Garland as Dorothy E. Gale.

in London, flying over the Atlantic Ocean to witness Garland's funeral in New York City five days later, then seeking out those ruby slippers in California and resting there until found and brought out into the limelight just months later to shine upon her fans once more. Just as *Harry Potter's* Lord Voldemort split his soul into pieces and set them to reside within meaningful inanimate objects, so too can we envision this dark force's attempt at immortality.

And now you're thinking this author is reaching. But before coming to any final judgments, consider this recent evidence regarding another rare and fateful piece of *The Wizard of Oz* memorabilia.

Among the items auctioned, sold on the side, or given away in the 1970 MGM Studios liquidation, was a blue-and-white gingham pinafore dress, the very dress worn by Judy Garland. It is just one of only four of the original costumes in existence and one of only two still including the white blouse. Quite reminiscent of the slippers.

The recipient of that dress, by Kent Warner's hand, no doubt, was Academy Award-winning actress Mercedes McCambridge. Oddly enough, McCambridge is credited with providing the voice for the demon Pazuzu in the 1973 movie *The Exorcist*. In that same year, McCambridge gifted the dress to a Catholic priest by the name of Father Gilbert Hartke. He ran the drama program at the Catholic University of America in Washington, D.C. at the time and had assisted McCambridge during her battles with alcoholism for many years. She was often hospitalized after episodes of heavy drinking.

It is unknown if the dress was ever used by the drama department, but it went missing for decades until well after Hartke's death in 1986. For nearly 50 years the dress lay, coincidently, in a shoebox inside a bag on top of a university faculty mailbox until a renovation of the school's Hartke Theatre revealed their existence.

After authentication, the university had planned on auctioning the dress through Bonhams auction house in New York. They estimated the dress is valued between $800,000 and $1.2 million. That was until Hartke's 81-year-old niece Barbara Hartke lawyered up and claimed the dress belongs to her. At the time of this publication, it was still undecided who won the rights to the dress.

A final tragedy befell McCambridge in 1987 when her son murdered his wife and two daughters then committed suicide. He blamed McCambridge.

Of Michael Shaw's experience, he was quoted in a phone interview with *Newsweek* as saying, "I have no desire to have them again. After years of bringing joy and happiness to so many thousands and thousands of people by being able to see them, now to me they're a nightmare." He ended the call by saying, "I'm not going to talk about it anymore. I'm sick of it. They're gone."

This author now feels the need to rewatch *The Wizard of Oz*. Maybe even re-read the original work by L. Frank Baum. Perhaps there are still unrecognized clues hiding among the words of that book, or in the film's stage scenery, or even in the glint of Judy Garland's eye as she promenaded down that yellow-brick road with her fantastical compatriots.

Maybe one of those images would lend some credibility to the ruby slippers being cursed. And maybe it would have been best if the shoes were never found at all. Some things are better left undisturbed.

They really are something. I bet you want to hold them now, don't you?
They might as well be made of real jewels.

A Chronology of Misery

Since L. Frank Baum published The Wonderful Wizard of Oz at the turn of the 20th century, numerous individuals, both real and fictional, have possessed or attempted to possess the magic shoes. When possessed with a pure heart the results were often benevolent. But in most cases those who coveted the world's most famous slippers suffered ill fortune. Below is a list of those whose lives have been touched by the slippers.

The Wicked Witch of the East
    Date: 1900 (book), 1939 (movie)
    Pair: The Witch's Pair (silver slippers in the book)
    Exposure: She owned them
    Impact: Died wearing them when Dorothy's house fell upon her

The Wicked Witch of the West
    Date: 1900 (book), 1939 (movie)
    Pair: None, but desired them over all else
    Exposure: Made multiple attempts to gain ownership through threats of violence, all failed
    Impact: Melted due to exposure by dihydrogen monoxide (water)

Dorothy Gale
   Date: 1900 (book), 1939 (movie)
   Pair: Every pair
   Exposure: Knew not of their nature and then only used them
to return home
   Impact: Reunited with family

Frances Gumm (Judy Garland)
   Date: 1939
   Pair: Every pair (some were used for dancing and others for
close-ups, and still others were test pairs)
   Exposure: Wore them for six months while working for MGM
Studios, never owned them
   Impact: Life-long addiction to drugs and alcohol, depression,
possible bipolar disorder, and suicidal tendencies resulting in an
early death at 47 years old

Gilbert Adrian
   Date: 1939
   Pair: Every pair
   Exposure: Designed the ruby slippers
   Impact: Went on to design costumes for a film entitled Possessed,
died at work of a fatal heart attack in 1959 at the age of 56

Roberta Bauman
   Date: 1940–1988
   Pair: Dorothy's shoes
   Exposure: Blessed little children and fans for many years by
showing them free of charge, sold at retirement
   Impact: Enjoyed early retirement and lived to be 86 years old

Kent Warner
   Date: 1970
   Pair: Every pair

Exposure: Found five pairs of ruby slippers in MGM's abandoned backlot, coveted one, sold the "Traveling Pair"

Impact: Died of AIDS in 1983 at the age of 41 years

Michael Shaw

Date: 1970–2005

Pair: The Traveling pair

Exposure: Used a traveling exhibition that charged fans to see the ruby slippers, charged museum to display the shoes

Impact: The ruby slippers were stolen from him. He was quoted as saying, "I have no desire to see them again." "I'm sick of it. They're gone." Lost many acquaintances due to his exposure.

Grand Rapids, Minnesota Police Department

Date: 2005–2018

Pair: None, but sought The Traveling pair

Exposure: Charged with finding the shoes and apprehending the perpetrators

Impact: Untold worthless leads, innumerable hours of futile detective work, only to have their efforts outshined by the FBI

Attorney Joseph Friedberg

Date: 2017

Pair: None, but negotiated for The Traveling pair

Exposure: Liaison (with Insabella) between an anonymous contact and the "holder of the shoes" in an effort to return the shoes to the public

Impact: Numerous hours of negotiations only to have his efforts stripped by an FBI sting

Retired Special Agent Michael Insabella

Date: 2017

Pair: None, but negotiated for The Traveling pair

Exposure: Liaison between Friedberg and his contacts in an

effort to return the shoes to the public

Impact: Months of stress resulting in health problems, an FBI search warrant to his premises, and the seizure of his personal belongings.

The United States Federal Bureau of Investigation

Date: 2017

Pair: The Traveling pair

Exposure: Has had possession since their seizure in a sting operation

Impact: False media representation, embarrassment of the department

~

The Life and Times of the "Traveling Pair" of Ruby Slippers

Of the five known pairs of slippers in existence, the "Traveling Pair" has seen the most action. Follow their tumultuous path through the timeline below.

1900

Author L. Frank Baum imagined the magical shoes as silver in his book entitled The Wonderful Wizard Oz.

1939

MGM costumer Gilbert Adrian created the iconic ruby slippers for Judy Garland to combat the new Technicolor lighting used in the motion picture The Wizard of Oz.

1970

Hollywood costumer Kent Warner discovers the shoes in an MGM backlot barn on the "3rd Floor – Ladies Character Wardrobe"

1970

Collector of silver screen mementos Michael Shaw purchased the slippers from Kent Warner privately for a sum of $2,500.

1970-2005

Michael Shaw owned the shoes and used them in a traveling showcase, hence their name.

2005

The "Traveling Pair" were stolen from the Judy Garland Museum in Grand Rapids, Minnesota by Kent Anderson and his accomplice "Carl."

2005-2017

The "Traveling Pair" of ruby slippers went on a mysterious adventure in which the details may very well be lost to time.

2017

A mysterious man approached Minneapolis lawyer Joe Friedberg with knowledge that a "holder of the shoes" possessed them and wished to cash in on the proposed award money.

2017-2018

Negotiations for the return of the ruby slippers took place with Joe Friedberg (representing the "holder of the shoes") and Retired Secret Service Agent Michael Insabella working together in communication with the insurance company and the Grand Rapids Police Department.

July 2018

During a sting operation in Minneapolis, Minnesota the shoes were seized by the FBI from the hands of Joe Friedberg who thought he was meeting with an insurance company representative. Friedberg went free, as did Insabella after his home was searched in vain on the same day.

Present Day

The "Traveling Pair" of ruby slippers is still in the possession of the Federal Bureau of Investigation at an undisclosed location. No information about the future of the shoes has been released by the organization.

Afterword

In early 2022, the FBI received a phone call from an elderly man reporting that he had information on the ruby slippers' theft. The man said he was willing to exchange this information for their assistance in keeping his girlfriend in the United States. The woman was in the country on a visa which was about to expire permanently.

The man was aware that the statute of limitations had run out on the theft of the shoes.

The FBI interviewed him. During the examination, he finally admitted it was he who had broken into the Judy Garland Museum and took the ruby slippers back in August 2005. He disclosed information that only a responsible party could have known. He stated that, in fact, Kent Anderson was the planner and his accomplice.

The FBI apparently bought this man's story. And the girlfriend remains in the U.S.

To this day, the FBI still has not furnished this new information to Michael Insabella, Joe Friedberg, or their attorneys. Nor have they granted letters of declination of prosecution to clear Insabella and Friedberg's names.

To date, none of Insabella's personal property has been returned, nor has he received a copy of the requested, but sealed, affidavit for search warrant of his residence.

From June 5 to June 13, 2022, Mike Insabella took his family, all

23 of them—children, grandchildren, and great-grandchildren—on a cruise to México and the Bahamas. Upon his return, he was telephoned by his attorney Robert Richman.

Richman had been contacted by Assistant United States Attorney Nicholas Chase, who had been handling this case, and asked if Insabella would be willing to cooperate in exchange for leniency.

Chase had apparently resigned from the U.S. Attorney's office and had taken a job as a state judge.

Insabella told Richman to tell Judge Chase, "Too late. You have not treated me fairly or with dignity. I can't tell you any more than I already have or that I have written. I've been transparent with you and the FBI since you came to my doorstep. I gave the FBI the passwords to my email accounts and flash drives. I haven't changed any of my passwords so the FBI would be able to maintain access to my online data.

"I don't intend to voluntarily speak or communicate with anyone from your office until my computer and flash drives are returned and the affidavit for search warrant from West Palm Beach is released.

"Where's my stuff?"

ADDENDUM

Sadly, Retired Secret Service Agent Michael R. Insabella passed away suddenly right before the publication of this work. The follwing is his obituary.

~

A life well-planned, well-lived, and well-loved.

Michael Rocco Insabella made his untimely departure from this world on the morning of July 31, 2022, only five days shy of his 75th birthday while recovering from a major surgery. Family and friends have shared an outpouring of love at his sudden passing describing him as strong, generous, compassionate, fun-loving, and a bit of a wise guy.

God broke the mold after Mike was born on August 5, 1947, in Newark, New Jersey. His father was Orazio "Harry" Insabella, a Navy Seabee and boilermaker, and his mother was Rosaria "Sally" Abbate, the ultimate loving Italian mother who retired after many years with the U.S. Postal Service. His parents, as well as his brother, Harry, and sister, Judy, have preceded him in death.

As a young boy, he learned how to play the piano and accordion. He performed at church, at family gatherings, and eventually with a doo-wop band called "The Epics." As an adult his musical gifts entertained at family gatherings and inspired similar gifts in his children and grandchildren.

In 1965, he graduated from Saint Joseph College Preparatory School. He maintained life-long friendships with many of his classmates known as the "Band of Brothers" who considered him the "class warrior," "a legend," and a "real stand-up guy!"

Next, he attended Biscayne College in Miami, known today as St. Thomas of Villanova, where he received a bachelor's degree in political science. One day, as he lay passed out on the beach slathered in iodine and baby oil, he was saved from 'heat exhaustion' by a surfing beauty named Toni who became his college sweetheart. They wed just before he graduated and were married for 32 years until she passed suddenly in 1998.

His first job out of college was as a patrol officer for the North Miami Beach Police Department. After three years there, Michael was hired in 1971 as a special agent with the Miami Field Office of the United States Secret Service. From there, he was part of the White House detail and protected Presidents Ford, Carter, and Reagan.

His service to the country and community didn't end there. Michael worked as a special agent in Miami, Florida, and Washington, D.C. He finished his career in the Albuquerque, New Mexico field office where he investigated counterfeit currency cases and worked undercover. He also acted as the chief liaison between the Secret Service and the FBI foreign and domestic terrorism cases, between the Sandia National Labs relating to the Strategic Defense Initiative and held top secret security clearance with compartmentalized clearance above top secret.

After 23 years of service, with retirement on the table, Michael started his own security consulting firm in 1994 called "MRI Associates." He was hired to do security planning for Presidential inaugurations as well as conventions, and other high-profile gatherings. A few years later, he became the Director of Executive Protection for Office Depot where he conducted security planning for the Chairman and CEO, and other corporate executives.

In 2017, Mike married Marion Calbough in Pico, Azores in the church where many generations of her family had wed. Her loving and playful nature quickly earned her the nickname "Mimi" and her healthy and adventurous spirit brought many extra years to Mike's life. They filled these years with loads of adventures including a honeymoon, with friends, across Europe and a four-month cruise around the world, while all along being sure to spend precious time with beloved friends and family.

In his spare time, Mike loved boating, saltwater fishing, snorkeling, diving, cooking, and helping others. Family, friends, and neighbors could always count on him to swoop in whenever they had a problem. He was always ready to suggest the best way (his way, of course!) to complete a task or provide a timeline, agenda, or directions to get things started. At the same time, he would roll up his sleeves and work tirelessly beside you to complete the job. In other words, rather than making 20 phone calls, everyone called Mike "The Fixer" because he always "had a guy" or in most cases, he was "the guy."

He enjoyed traveling and recently said he had "been everywhere he ever wanted to go and seen everything he ever wanted to see." He was looking forward to sharing his love of travel with family. In June of 2022, Mike gathered 23 members of his family for a Caribbean adventure. During this cruise he had the opportunity to dance, sing, dine, reminisce, and bond with everyone. This included his wife, four children, eight grandchildren, and three great-grandchildren. He later referred to this as "one of the greatest events of my life."

He leaves behind his wife, Marion Insabella, of Jensen Beach, Florida, three daughters: Annamarie Insabella Schaeffer of Jupiter, Florida, Andria Insabella Keene of Boynton Beach, Florida, and Angela Insabella Dean of Jupiter, Florida, and his son Michael A. Insabella of Rockwall, Texas. He relished his role as "Grandpa Mike" and "Papo" and will be remembered for his Cordovox dance parties, stubble-tickling kisses, occasionally inappropriate stories and sing-alongs, machine gun sound effects, and advice about always remembering "Rule #1." His grandchildren include Brianna Byers and Britany Lovins, Jeffrey and Toni Keene, Adalyn, Laynie, and Michael Rocco Insabella, his namesake, and Jonah P. Dean. His great-grandchildren are Olivia, Mason, and Jack Lovins.

Acknowledgements

The author wishes to first thank the contributors—anonymous or otherwise revealed in the pages of this book—to this production for the gracious opportunity to work alongside them on such a worthy endeavor. I'm exceedingly pleased that together we could accomplish the goals set before us and bring to light a worthy record of events.

Appreciation goes to my wife, Andria, for her unyielding support and informative handwritten commentaries throughout the daunting editing process.

Without my fellow writers at Word Weavers International, my skill as a writer would never be good enough for my deserving readers. Thank you, brothers and sisters, for your advice.

Finally, as always, I give gratitude to God for His unending inspiration, guidance, and gift of patience.

Works Cited

"Materials characterization of the Ruby Slippers from the 1939 classic film, *The Wizard of Oz*," 07 November 2018, Heritage Science.

The Slippers. Directed by Morgan White, Tricon Films and Television, 2016

Expedition Unknown, Hunt for the Ruby Slippers. Performance by Josh Gates. Season 5, Episode 7. 2018.

Treasure! The Search for the Ruby Slippers. Written and produced by Rhys Thomas. Narrated by Stuart Nelson. A&E, 1998.

Ramchandani, A. and Darby, S. June 15, 2021 to August 3, 2021. *No Place Like Home*, C13 Originals.

About the Author

Let it be common knowledge that Jeff Keene II is the son-in-law of the late Mr. Michael R. Insabella.

Keene holds degrees in biology, chemistry, and linguistics. His writing path began when a high school teacher assigned him the task of creating an original screenplay. Twenty-five years later, that screenplay was published as a short story in a Long Island historical society's newsletter. But the writing bug really began when developing a textual criticism about a New Testament story in a master's level seminary course in 2012. Since then, he's had the undying urge to write about unnamed characters in the Bible who've met Jesus.

Keene has served as a volunteer firefighter in New York where he suffered a line-of-duty injury resulting in the loss of his right foot below-the-knee. He has worked on a NOAA scientific research vessel for 17 days at sea and even applied to NASA's Teacher in Space program. He currently serves as a public school teacher.

Keene lives with his wife, Andria, in South Florida. They have two adult children, both studying in the fine arts.

Connect with Jeff Keene II at:
https://peglegpenman.com

Also Available From

WordCrafts Press

Pericope
by Jeff Keene II

Geezer Stories: The Care & Feeding of Old People
by Laura Mansfield

Against Every Hope: India, Mother Teresa, and a Baby Girl
by Bonnie Tinsley

Before History Dies
by Jacob Carter

Truth, Lies & Alzheimers
by Lisa Skinner & Doublas Collins

www.wordcrafts.net